FOREX TRADING FOR BEGINNERS

*The Ultimate Comprehensive Guide
For Any Forex Aspirant, Top Trading
Strategies, How to Make the Right
Investment and Make Money Online!
Create Wealth in 2021 and Beyond...*

information contained within this document, including, but not limited to, — errors, omissions, or inaccuracies.

TABLE OF CONTENTS

Chapter 1

Understanding Forex: Getting To Know The Basics

"I don't know what Forex is, and since I don't understand what it is, I'm sure I haven't participated in that yet." – this is something that you might have heard from yourself, or from someone you've known. When something appears or sounds strange, it is quite natural for people to frown upon it, or avoid talking about it.

But the truth is, if you have already visited other countries, then you already took part in it. Forex is obviously just a shorter term for "Foreign Exchange." Even though it sounds really simple, the logistics behind it are actually broader and much more interesting, especially if you're the type of individual who wants to make the most out of your earnings while just staying at home.

To make it easy for a layman to understand the complexity that Forex might spell, it can just be perceived as a major business institution where money from various places around the world are traded from one form into another. We might say that whenever money transcends across other national borders, it needs to be converted into something else so it can be useful.

It is dubbed as "The world's biggest financial market," which makes it clear that it really does contribute a lot to the over-all flow of the world's economy. Within its virtual halls, great amounts of money are transacted, traded, and dealt with by a lot of huge business entities as well as average persons. And we're not only talking about millions of Dollars here, but trillions of Dollars, Euros, and almost any other global currencies you can think of.

The exchange of currencies that take place within Forex is very crucial for the international business world. Forex enthusiasts and participants range from government institutions to private corporations, to plain individuals like you and me. Governments are known to utilize the power of Forex for the furthering of their country's interests.

For instance, when a particular country wants to conduct some business deals with other countries such as in lending money, borrowing funds, or even in giving aid whenever crises arise, a country needs to convert its existing currency into foreign currency.

With business entities, they leverage the Forex market to facilitate business deals within the international trade. While they do so, they might need to convert the value of goods and services in exchanging payments from customers into the currencies they prefer.

Individual investors, or those that we call ordinary traders also use Forex as they monitor the rise and flow of global currencies. In just a span of a week, or even in just a few days, currency prices my hit really high or hit really low, mainly because the market doesn't sleep.

Though it is just open from Monday to Friday, it functions round-the-clock during those days, conducting a day's business starting at 4:00 pm central time and ends at the same time the day after. Forex operates this way because it encompasses the demands and activities of the global economy.

How Forex Trading Can Change Your Life

Trading is one of the best money-making trends in the world these days. It is here to stay and will mostly likely be even more attractive and marketable in the next decades. According to the data given by Brokernotes, one of the most recognizable trading publication websites on the web, there are 9.6 million people around the world that are joining the online trading bandwagon.

It means that for every 781 people you meet, there is one of them that's actually doing some trading on a regular basis. Now, with online technologies become more advanced with each passing month, that figure could rise even higher in the next few years. People's lives are changed because of the trading habits… it would be unwise of you to not join the fray.

Now let's tackle another important question, "How much can you really earn with Forex trading?"

To have a rough but simple idea, let's take a look at the success of this very popular Wall-Street guy named Marty Schwartz. He is dubbed as "The Pitbull," and with good reason. Why? Because he has one of the highest levels of aggression, when it comes to investing in Forex.

He is not only about plain attack though, because he is very methodical and smart with his decisions. He has an estimated income of 25% per month. So if he invested a million Dollars in a particular moment, it would mean that he will be twice as rich in the next 4 months.

You can be as rich as him… if you set your mind into believing that you can, and if you work on your trading skills and decisions. That can happen of course if you take the time to perform these 3 very important things: practice, practice, and practice.

Compared to other forms and methods of investments, Forex really pays a lot more. For instance, typical banks will just give you an increase of 2% per year. Mutual funds reward you higher, for it gives 10% per year. The same happens in the stock market. Even if all 3 forces get combined, they are still low compared to the 25% increase that Forex gives. Forex is the ultimate champion, so to speak.

But you may say, Mr. Schwartz might have been a rich guy already before he participated in Forex. He already got a big capital at his disposal already even before he got interested with currency exchange.

While that might be true, you have to know that many people have been through a story that we can really call as a "rags to riches tale." Forex really is a life-changer, and it is for the following reasons:

It can make you obtain great amounts of money, in the a very short time.

That's how attractive Forex trading can really be. Some traders put in a certain amount say, 100 Dollars. By trading wisely and carefully, many of the are able to double that amount in just an hour, or even in a few minutes. Some who invested on thousands of dollars are also able to triple that amount in also just a few hours. Needless to say, some of them became millionaires in just a matter of weeks.

It can give you huge returns of investment, with just very little effort.

When you engage in trading, all you will be doing is the act of staring at charts, picking up news about the market, make decisions and implement a set of trading actions. You wait for a while, and then your money increases in value, even though you were just sitting down, at the confines of your own home. Some people's idea of getting rich means you have to invest on real physical capital and work in real workplaces. But as a Forex trader, you will achieve the same level of wealth even though the physical effort your pouring out is just a minuscule one.

It is a safer, better version of gambling.

Truth to be told, Forex trading is every bit as similar to gambling in a casino. You place your bet, and wait for how the dice may fall, or where the arrows may point to. It is a very addictive kind of activity. But here's the good thing about it, it's not as harmful as gambling, and not as illegal as the most common forms of gambling are, when they are placed in unregulated places. This is not to say that gambling is really a bad thing, it's just that with Forex trading, you're not only helping yourself, but you are also contributing to the profits that the global market can accumulate.

Upon reading the above statements, you're getting very excited, and that's very understandable. But here's something that you should know: Forex trading really can in fact make you the richest person in the neighborhood, but before you reach that position, you need to undergo through a series of self-education, risk-taking, and failure absorption – all of which are not easy sets of undertakings

The 3 major advantages of Trading stated above are now contradicted within the same chapter of this book, and perhaps, you're starting to get mad. But Forex trading is not as easy as it may appear to your ears, it is for this reason that writings of this kind exists, because trading really can be difficult, but it can be made to appear easy, if you have the initiative and bravery needed for such an endeavor.

To motivate you even further, let's take a peek at the life of Daniel Martin. During his younger years, he was a Migrant in London. The bad thin about him during those times is that he can't speak English, even in little doses.

Fast forward to the future however, he has amassed some popularity within the field of Forex trading. While he is not to boast of his exact earnings, he has one been given with this cool tagline which is "Turning The 2020 Crash Into $222,000 Cash."

That might not be as big as the amount that Mr. Schwartz is earning, but Mr. Martin's story can make us say that plain, ordinary people like you and me can be greatly changed my Forex. It just goes to show that even without millions at our disposal, we can get a truly attainable set of earnings by just trading strategically.

Mr. Martin's formula for success is declared by himself as 95% psychology, 4% capital, and 1% action. This means that what you need at a greatest measure is how you set your mind into doing what needs to be done. In that case, let's delve into the topic deeper.

How Forex Trading Really Works

Maybe the statements above are still too vague, or maybe it's too technical for you. Let's break the definition down in the simplest analysis possible.

Here's a simple example of basic foreign exchange activity:

Let's say a certain company buys a bulk of products from another country. To make the purchase happen, the company owner needs to acquire some currency for that country first, just like when you go on vacations and holiday trips. The only notable difference is that the exchange of amounts that take place are just in a greater scale.

When that company goes through the process of exchanging of those amounts, they contribute to the changing the corresponding prices of those products as well as anything related to it.

When there are more people who actively use a form of currency, the demand for that currency also increases. When the demand decreases, so does the price of the products – it is one of the core concepts of business that everyone can understand easily. With all of these exchanges happening all over the world, the exchange rates constantly move.

Like in any market, the price of any currency is based on the laws of supply and demand. For instance, if there are more people or business entities who exchange Euros into Dollars, the price of the Dollar will rise in comparison to the price of the other, which will change the exchange rate.

Here's a much simpler example that we can see every day so that we can clearly understand how anyone can benefit from foreign currency trades:

Let's say a guy named Greggy lives in Europe and went on a vacation in the US. The guy would certainly bring some European cash with him, and will surely exchange it with some Dollars. During his stay in the US.

Now, let's say Greggy exchanged his 1000 Euros into US currency with a rate of 2.8 Dollars for every Euro. He would get 1400 USD. Let's assume he didn't spend that money, and brought it back to his hometown in Europe, and have managed to keep the money until the exchange rate dropped to 2.8. Instead of getting back his original amount which is 1000, he would actually gain 77 Euros more, so he will now have a total of 1077 due to the lower value that the US Dollar got during that time.

He gained additional earnings just for holding on to a currency that he obtained from a foreign land. That is how Forex basically works – just the simple act of exchanging one form of currency to another, from a certain country to another country, and vice versa.

A trader or investor buys one form of currency, holds on to it for a while, wait for the rates to rise, and then make the move to change his money back, increasing earnings along the way. When to do the exact act of trading is what makes Forex trading very tricky. It can be really hard if you are just starting out. But with careful analysis and repetitive investing, you will find it very easy over time.

Based on what you have understood so far, you might begin to think that traveling from one country to another can actually make you richer than you ever were. In that sense, you are correct... but expert traders would advise you against that. Unless of course if you really love to travel and visit different places.

Aside from the fact that traveling from country to country can be truly burdensome, it isn't also very practical, especially with the current global health crisis we're experiencing today. Thankfully though, there is a much easier alternative to trading foreign currencies – doing it with online means.

Today, many people are getting richer by the minute as they tap into the existence of internet entities called "Forex Brokers." By working with such online businesses, you can take advantage of the rise and fall of foreign currencies right at the screen of your laptop, or even your phone.

Just like what that guy Greggy experienced as he traveled from Europe to the US, you can trade one currency into another and make your earnings significantly higher as you witness the fluctuations of currencies all over the world. Trading within the Forex market via the internet has lots of great advantages.

In addition to the convenience of doing it within the confines of your own home, you can also take advantage of the idea that Forex never sleeps. This means that you can do some trading activities at absolutely any time of your convenience, though you can just do it 5 days a week.

To participate in it, you don't even have to procure a really huge budget. For the moment, you can just start with just as little as 10 USD. Some say it could be as low as 5. You can't expect it to grow really big though. However, you can use that amount as some sort of "trading startup and practice" money.

To be truly successful with Forex Trading, you need to invest not only in a certain monetary amount but in a huge portion of your time as well. Success with money matters is not a walk in the park. You need to learn, take risks, and improve on your methods and techniques. Rich people, as well as anyone who has attained success in all areas of life, attained their royalties because of patience and hard work. You as a Forex beginner should not be any different at all.

The Mathematics and Logistics Behind Currency Exchange

Here's something that you should really accept in becoming a Forex trader: You have to be great in Math. This is not to discourage you, it's just something that you have to be good at so you can be truly profitable with this new undertaking you're considering.

Do you need to learn complex Math? No. Actually, what you need is just very simple mathematics – the set of Math that can make you understand basic numerical operations and some understanding about decimals. If you're good enough with that already, then we shouldn't have any problem at all.

Successful traders are not all excellent mathematicians, however all of them are people who really love working with numbers. They might not be that good with Algebra or anything similar, but they are the kind of people who can think mathematically in the most efficient manner. As a Forex neophyte, do your very best to adapt to that skill – it's the best and only way so you can proceed smoothly with your trading journey.

Now, let's hop into the typical act of trading. Whenever you do business with Forex, you're not only dealing with one currency, but 2 currencies at the same time. Such an intertwining is called a "currency pair." The main concept of gaining or losing revolves around the value of 1 currency in comparison to another.

Comparing and trading currencies can be easily understood by putting them side by side, or by looking at them from left to right. Let's break down a simple example of pairing the most popular currencies ever: Dollars and Euro. When the "Euro to US Dollar pairing" is equal to 1.20, it means that your 1 Euro will be converted into 1.20 if you do some trading at that particular moment.

For another pairing, let's say the US Dollar to Canadian Dollar pairing is equal to 1.25. It also means that your 1 Dollar will also be raised to 1.25 if you trade it with that currency from Canada. Even though there are 2 currencies involved in a trading act, they act like a single currency from the eyes of the Forex market itself. Just like in investing on a particular stock, an investor will gain some profit when he buys a currency pair. When the value of those currencies rise, so does his investment.

Another way investors make money is through speculation. For instance, if an investor feels that the economy of Europe will rise way faster than that of the US, it will make him believe that the Euro will have more power than the US Dollar. The investor will then buy the Euro-Dollar pairing based on his analysis. If that pairing's value becomes high, he will gain money. Conversely, when the value of the Euro-Dollar drops, he will lose some of his earnings.

Now, let's dig a little deeper into the main key aspects of the Forex market. Let's talk about the term called "Margin." When you trade using this method, it means you will only put up a certain percentage of the total investment given by a Forex Broker. The amount you need for that is often called "Margin Requirement."

There is also this term called Stock. With it, you are allowed to borrow funds from your Forex broker. However, trades can only be covered using your existing Forex account. This means that a new investor can't borrow funds to begin. A newbie trader needs to put in some funds into a newly created Forex account. Only then can he start trading.

In using the Margin method, you have to be aware that how much you can earn is dependent on the value of the currency pairings and the price of the trade that's taking place. The size of a pair is basically called "Lot." The most notable sub-categories for this are standard lot, and mini lot. A standard lot is known to carry a value of 100,000 units, while a mini lot has 10,000 units.

Depending on you broker firm's policies, you may also start with just 1,000 units. Such a value is called a "micro-lot." The value of a Margin requirement can be as small as just 2% of the total investment or it could be as large as 20%. But for most trading activities, the average margin requirement falls within the 3 to 5% range.

Let's understand how margin requirement value is calculated with another example. Let's say the pairing of Euro-Dollar has the equivalent of 2.40 and is invested with 2 standard lots. That should make us calculate 2.40 x 200,000, resulting into a capital of 480,000 Dollars. That's a huge amount, one that can surely make you acquire big profits along the way.

The good thing is that you don't really need to pay that exact amount so you can begin trading. What you really have to pay is just the margin requirement. If it's value is just 5%, then you will only need to pay 2400 Dollars.

From that concept, another term called "leverage" should be introduced. It is something that enables an investor to control a huge amount with just a small value of money. We can say that if an investor has 120,000 Dollars, he can control that with just an amount of 3,600 Dollars because it's the 3% of the real amount – the actual value of the margin requirement.

The existence of the leverage method is one of the most important elements of the Forex market, as many analysts claim. But many experts also claim that it is one of the biggest risks investors may come across. It may give an investor the highest earning potential, but conversely, it can also make way for the greatest of losses.

Whenever a trading act happens within Forex, we have to remember that there are 2 currencies involved each time. And as stated above, the 2 is actually viewed as just one. It means that while you're lending 1 currency of the pair, you're also borrowing on the other side.

Such an activity is what the lending rate policies of a certain country is really all about. To sum all of the technicalities up, we can just arrive into the understanding that the entirety of the trading within the Forex market is this: when the value of 1 country's currency goes high, the currency of another country goes low.

By taking advantage of such kinds of events, a Forex investor can be a very big winner in the shortest time imaginable. Consequently though, a careless trader could also become the biggest loser of all time.

Forex Then and Now: How Forex Has Changed Due To Technological Breakthroughs

If we take a look back in history, we would understand that because of the existence of technology and the ease and comfort it gives, the underlying processes that revolve around money are also revolutionized. Just after a few generations when the concept of money has been transformed into paper bills, the act of money-making and investing has changed dramatically as well.

Because going to the bank has become too burdensome for people as well as for the bank owners themselves, they invented "wire-transfer technology" – a process in which transferring of funds can already be done via-electronic signals, which can also be reinforced by telephone conversations.

There also came the Automated Teller Machine, which really offered a great convenience for anyone who wants to avoid the hassle of bringing large amount of real physical cash on their wallets with them.

But such methods were revolutionized even further, because apparently, the business world as well as the people within it are working non-stop in a really speedy way to get things done much simpler and easier. As a result, monetary transactions are now executable on the internet which greatly changed everything.

Gone are the days when you need to actually travel into another country just so you can participate in currency exchange. In the past, people need to be physically present in trading and money-exchanging firms so they can have their foreign money changed. With the existence of computers in homes and offices, transactions became more accessible via keyboard strokes and mouse clicks.

And what's more amazing is that today, such activities can already be done within the comforts of just nearly everywhere. Apparently, mobile technology hasn't only changed the way we communicate, but on how we use and view money as well. People nowadays, even those that belong to the lowliest of the lows, can actually use their cellphones as their wallets.

Furthermore, many online portals are providing tools and apps that can make financial transactions much easier even for the not-so-rich individuals. Also, many experienced traders are sharing their knowledge and expertise within video streaming sites like Youtube. Truly, there is no excuse for anyone who claims that Forex trading is hard, and only for the ones with a silver platter handed over to them since birth.

About the online trading platforms mentioned earlier, literally all of them offer great assistance in helping anyone who's new to modern-day trading. Some of them even offer "trading mimicry options" in which all a novice trader needs to do is just copy the trading activities of an experienced trader.

By just clicking on a button or an a certain link, the trading methods and exact actions of that trader will manifest on your trading acts too. It means that if that trader wins it hugely, then so will you, although your actual profit will be dependent only on the amount you invested.

That goes to say of course that if that trader loses, you will lose too. But the point of the matter is, trading is really so much easier these days because you can choose to copy the trading practices of successful Forex investors who rarely fail.

Such benefits are widely available these days, which can help us arrive with the conclusion that with Forex, your financial worries can really vanish… if you have the right motivation and mindset to trek into the amazing path of digital trading. If you want to learn the most effective means by which you can make a living out of Forex Trading, sit back and read on.

Starting Forex Trading

Knowing the basic requirements so you can start your first Forex adventures.

First, you have to be within the "legal-age bracket." This means that if you're lower than 18, you can't do some trading just yet. Sorry kids, you're gonna have to grow up for a few more years before you can get rich with the Forex market.

The cool thing though is even if you're a kid, you can make a "practice account" in which you'll have the benefit of enjoying some "Forex play money." When you are already old enough and have gained some knowledge and experience already, you can then use that to your advantage later in adulthood.

Another thing to have is your valid ID. Government-issued IDs could really come in handy in this requirement. You can also use your driver's license, your passport, or whatever ID card that can declare proof of your real identity. You need these as pertinent documents so that your presence in the Forex world can be validated.

You also need proof of your address. Those billing sheets about your electric bills, water bills, and similar related documents should be ideal enough as they can give sufficient proof that you really are a resident of a certain area of your town. Or you can just get a residency clearance from your government municipality's office, that should also be good enough.

You also need to have a bank account, or some of those platforms that can hold digital accounts for your finances such as Paypal, Skrill, or Stripe. There are so many of them out there. What you just have to bear in mind is that almost all of the long-running platforms that are similar to the ones mentioned can be a really good storage area for your Forex earnings.

For the equipment needed, your smartphone will do. You may also use a laptop, a desktop PC, as long as they are connected to the internet. You will then use such devices to connect to the online Forex brokers that are practically just very easy to find.

Before you begin with your trading journey, you need to make sure that you are prepared to lose. Although Forex can really make you extremely rich in just a few moments, it can also make you more broke than you ever were in your life. Speaking of losing, you need to pay attention to the following.

Dealing With Failure: Reasons Why An Aspiring Forex Trader Will Fail

If you want to be truly successful as a currency trader, avoid the following mistakes by all means:

Not having enough understanding of the market.

Truthfully, no mistake is bigger than this. Successful traders, regardless of their area of expertise be it cryptocurrency, the stock market, Forex, or any other similar realms you could think of having this thing that they call their "domain of confidence." As they go about what they do like choosing new forms of investments, collaborating with like-minded people, and making decisions, they stay on that domain.

As they stay within that area of business where they plan to make huge amounts of income, they do their very best to learn about it because they know it for themselves that the best way to be successful with the business, you have to really understand how the structure of the business works.

Most Forex newbies approach the business as just a simple piece of object that they can plug themselves into and hope that money will just flow through their wallets. Such people think that by simply sticking themselves into the business without doing anything, they can get rich easily. If you're that type of person, then there's no hope for you as a Forex trader.

So the main emphasis of this first item is that before you proceed with the real mechanisms of Forex trading, do your homework and do some reconnaissance like that of a highly trained assassin. Although you won't be killing anybody within the business, you really need to truly grasp and understand what is Forex, and how it really works.

Not having a solid and actionable plan.

Since trading is a very serious undertaking, you need to really come up with a solid plan and have the guts and the rock-solid willingness to put those plans into action. The natural reaction for novice investors when hearing about something that can increase their income is this: they put in some money, expect it to grow, and just wait for that quick moment in which they can siphon their earnings into their wallets and bank accounts.

Many newbie investors are having that mindset within themselves, and it is exactly why most of them fail miserably. Some of them also think about retiring early, having some passive income generators, and doing things just to enjoy themselves.

While such plans are good things to execute, it would be a really bad idea to just think about that end scenario without really laying out some solid plans. Some of them don't even think deeply about the proper amounts of money that they need for those plans, thinking that things will just fall into place automatically.

Most newbie investors in Forex are too excited about the money they can earn and are willing to trek into new money-making territory like blind men walking near a cliff. Such a notion is really bad and not to mention a very dangerous idea. So here's what you should do, take a pen and a paper, write down your plans, think about them deeply, and take intense and strategic actions in doing them when you are ready enough already.

Unwillingness to invest time within the market.

All things exist because of 2 important elements: space and time. Ask any physicist, and all of them would surely agree with the statement. Income is a very good thing to have, no argument about that. But thinking about income and actually having income are 2 very different things.

No matter how good you are at dreaming about the physical objects that you can buy with your income, and about how you will store those piles of income, all such thinking and planning will not amount to anything, if you don't invest in a very crucial element: time.

Forex trading is one of the most sought-after activities conducted and engaged in by the richest people in the world today. Do you want to know why they're so good and why they're so successful at what they do? It is because they put a lot of time into learning about the thing, and doing the thing constantly and repeatedly until they become masters at the art of trading and investing within the Foreign Exchange Market.

Successful traders do not only invest in money matters, but they also invest in time because they want to learn. The good thing about Forex investing is that it's never too late for anyone to start investing. Even if you're already past your prime or even if you're within the "senior age bracket," you can still have a profitable trading journey ahead of you.

You might not be as young and energetic as those teenagers who are now getting so good within Forex (Yes, there are very successful youngsters in their late teens who are well-known within the Forex market. We will talk about them later if you keep on reading.), but you have one decisive power that those kids don't have: the wisdom of an experienced man.

Even though you are not yet well-versed with the art of trading currencies yet, you are most likely experienced with other things from other areas of life. You can then apply those experiences in your trading undertakings. Those kids might have the energy, but you have the advantage of wisdom and experience as you have lived certainly longer than all of them.

Doing a lot of wrongful buying practices.

Everyone makes mistakes. And in order to really learn, it is understood that errors and wrong decisions will be made along the way. But if you can prevent those errors from taking place in the first place, why not utilize such an advantage? This is something that most Forex newbies should really put into the highest of considerations.

When you are about to embark on your first trading steps, you will surely be lured and tempted to buy currency pairings that appear to be very cheap but are actually so overpriced. For instance, when looking at Forex charts, which you will surely do if you want to get serious with the business, you might see the rise and fall of monetary value in an erroneous way.

Oftentimes, newbies would surely get excited when there is a sudden rise of a particular currency when compared to another currency and will quickly jump into the trading act, not realizing that they could earn a lot more, if they waited for just a longer bit of time.

Conversely, one of the most common mistakes among newbies is the desire to earn more when the rise of a currency's value is actually the highest that it can get at a given moment. The trick to getting around to this is to play within the mid-level approach: don't get too greedy, but don't be too slow either.

To simply put it, invest in ample time to learn the basics, and improve on them with thorough practice. As you do them more and more each time, you will have the wisdom that can be equated with the most successful Forex traders within the market today.

Not having the proper mental conditioning about trading

If put the advice of Daniel Martin's into high consideration, then we need to really set our minds properly into the game of trading. Some very strong warriors are known to lose to inferior fighters because of one thing: they lack the proper mindset needed to win the battle. Being victorious, even in the aspect of physical fighting is not only about having a strong body, but about having a strong will too.

Now, if you are not someone who has the iron will to step into the digital halls of the trading world and have the guts to win or to lose, you'll never get anywhere near the avenues success. During your first trading actions, you will surely have the initial feelings of getting overwhelmed, that's natural. But in the midst of that, you need to rise above the very moment of sinking and get yourself to the top quickly.

What you really need to do is to learn to balance impulse with patience, greed with wit, and quickness with tarrying – those are natural manifestations of all businessmen. You have get along with that pretty well… it's the only way by which you can step into the first doorsteps of financial success.

Getting Into The Real Action: The Trading Tasks That A Forex Newbie Must Undergo

We've discussed the concepts that revolved around Forex already, and we've had enough statements that should have motivated us to delve deeper into the business. Now, Let's get right into the real action. Let's get into the "nitty-gritty" so to speak.

Without further ado, let's talk about what you really need to do and undergo as you go about your trading tasks each and every day of your dear existence? Wait a minute, every day? Yes, my friend, every day.

Successful Forex traders, as well as any kind of businessmen for that matter, became very well-seasoned and extremely popular at what they do because of one thing: they really love what their profession, and they deal with their business so religiously that missing a single day with their routine would make them feel like they're sick with a very infectious diseases.

Of course, they take breaks from time to time and go on vacations occasionally because after all, what good is money if you can't spend it? But as soon as they're back from their strolls and their tours, they once again deal with their business with the deepest and most intense of seriousness.

You as a Forex neophyte should condition yourself to do the same too. Now, let's get into the real action.

As stated in the earliest discussions, Forex revolves around the idea of exchanging one country's money for another country's money, that's just the simple framework of the business. No magic there, that's just it. Now the real question would be attaining the desired profit you can get from it. Beginners are often scared about taking the first steps.

Don't get too scared though, because there are actually brokers who will lend you a starting amount like 30 Dollars, that you can use as your starting investment. If in any case, you will not gain anything from that, you will not be liable to pay anything. Pretty cool right? But if you are successful with your first trade though, you will pay that amount. It's a win-win for both parties, and people have been taking advantage of that already.

You can participate in Forex for free. You can just visit the website freeforexmoneynodeposit.com and you'll be given a 30-Dollar practice money that you can use for your first Forex adventures. Aside from the free goodie that you can have, there is also a tutorial video there that will guide you on how to create and open a Forex account.

You might ask this, "Who gives away money for free just so more money can be attained?" Nobody can blame you if you won't believe that some people would actually give that amount totally for free. But here's the truth about that… it's simply advertising, some kind of propaganda.

If you visit that web page, you will see that there are 4 internet firms there that are actually brokers. By choosing to tap into them for your first Forex trades, they are actually announcing to the world that they are among the best Forex brokers that you can trust.

30 Dollars is just a small amount for them, even if there are lots of us who will take advantage of it.

It's actually a win for them. Because it is a very clever way of advertising their Brokerage's existence.

One of the most popular brokers among beginners is XM. Should you choose it, you can begin with as low as 5 Dollars from your debit card or 20 Dollars via online banking. The good thing about XM is that it has zero-fee policy for withdrawing your earnings. It is actually one of the most appealing things about XM.

The reason why Forex offers an increase that high is actually due to the fact that each and every day, its market gains around 5 trillion Dollars. This means that the more active you are with your participation within the Forex market, the more you can actually gain a huge portion of that 5 trillion.

It is the total amount shared among Forex investors with each passing day. Statistically speaking, all the stock markets in the world combine are still a little thing compared to the entirety of the Forex market.

Now, about that free 30-Dollar capital for Forex trading, would that be good enough? For someone who has no solid knowledge yet, absolutely. Now suppose you want to hit it big, or if you want to do some real, big-enough trading, You need to use your bank account on that aspect.

You need to siphon some big-enough amount into your chosen Forex broker so you can expect to have higher returns too. But if you want to just have a feel of what trading really is all about, you can just experiment with that free 30.

Any bank account you may have, as long as those banks are engaged in online banking can be used for all your trading adventures. All of them for sure have online connectivity of some sort. Which bank doesn't? Nothing, right? So you can choose any bank at all. Or you can use those digital financial account platforms mentioned earlier too. You can actually just use any of those at your convenience.

Once you hop into your first act of trading, one of the most crucial things you need to figure out is the importance of the word "low." Why? Because your very first Forex deed must be this: buying a currency at its lowest possible value. This is just like buying a very cheap and affordable product that will be very useful for your metaphorical store when the time is right to sell it.

As you should have understood already by now, a time will come when the value of that currency you bought will rise high, way higher than the price when you originally bought it, that will be the best time to let go of that piece of monetary commodity, which will then usher in your very first Forex earnings.

The profit you'll get will not be at a constant rate because as what's told previously, the value of a certain currency can really rise and fall… sometimes unpredictably. Just bear in mind that whenever you engage in a Forex trading act, you will be buying and selling at the same time. Think of it as being on a see-saw: You and a playmate will experience a rising and a falling, not at the same exact second, but throughout the entire time when the 2 of you are see-sawing for enjoyment.

Now speaking of the see-saw act, there will be that specific moment when you get the high-ground position. In Forex trading, if you see the value of a currency rising really high, and you have this feeling that it will drop in the next moments, then it will be the best time for you to sell that currency – that is where you can get your much-awaited income from.

Let's have a simple example. Let's say you bought a currency that's priced at 5.50 and after a few hours, its value has become 7. If you decide to sell it at that moment, it means that you gained 1 and a half of that currency. By waiting for a few hours, you can really earn more, many traders are so good with it that they become so much richer in just a very short span of time.

But as a beginner, you should not risk it too much. Having a little earning during your first tries is so much better than having no earnings at all, or worse yet, losing your money due to some bad decisions. This should make us think about…

The Risks And Dangers In Doing Your First Trading Acts

The concept of losing money as a trader can be simply understood by looking at an event that often takes place within the currency world. Sometimes a currency starts to depreciate. Like for instance, the price of the US Dollar compared to an Asia currency like the Philippine peso could drop relative to each other. Sometimes, it is priced at 50 Php while sometimes it could be 48, or even lower.

The same goes with other currencies out there. As an aspiring trader, you really need to watch out for such trends. Don't worry too much though, there is an easy way to get get the hang of this problem. There are actually mental conditioning drills that you can implement on yourself so that such an exhausting chore will be a bit easier for beginners like you.

So if you're a Filipino and you're seeing that the value of Pesos is at an all-time low for a set of weeks, it would be easy to say that it's a bad time to go to the US. Because your money, which is of course so much lower compared to the currency of that country, will be pushed even lower once you do some exchanging there.

But when you see that the value of the Peso compared to the Dollar is priced at around 50 or a bit higher, then we can say that it would be a good time to visit your American friends. Don't expect the Peso to be even close to 60 though, such an event couldn't happen for now, at least, not yet anyway.

But when trading with currencies such as the Japanese Yen, or the Euro, that is where you can get the best profits possible. There will be more discussions about such currency lists a little later.

Aside from talking about highs and lows and rising and falling, let's talk about liquids. Like water? Like oil? Like alcohol? Something like that, but a different kind of liquid. Known for their characteristic of being "incompressible," they are highly of use to the processes that govern this dear world of ours. So how are they related to the Forex market?

In a lot of ways, they are highly relevant. Because when we study liquids, we can figure out the volatility of the events around us... including what goes on within the money-making and money-trading field. We see oceans rise and fall as tides get controlled by the moon. And if we acknowledge it, changes in the water will rise all boats or sink all of them.

Another relevance about liquid as a term in the Forex market is the "liquidity" that you can execute as you go around buying and selling currencies. Whenever you are interested to buy a particular currency, you can execute that plan at will. All it takes is just a few seconds, or even just a single second, provided of course that the internet connection in which your phone or computer is attached to, is quite stable and reliable.

Knowing The Best Time For Trading

The Forex market works round the clock, 5 days a week, you knew that already. Does it mean you can do some trading and make money any time of the day as long as they fall within that 5-day scope? Yes. However, you also need to be aware of the most ideal times of trading so that you can make some really good choices and decisions about the exact currency you need to buy or trade for.

To understand the paragraph above, we have to grasp some understanding about Greenwich Mean Time. It is a system by which time zones all over the world are cohesively weaved together so the events that take place within them can be recorded accordingly and appropriately. Tourism, as well as currency exchange rely heavily on time zone schedules so they can conduct business in the smoothest ways possible.

Why do we need to know about it? Because it will give you a better understanding of how the Exchange market really works on a global scale, as a business that never sleeps. Forex experts claim that from the perspective of the GMT time zone, the 3 major components of the market operate according to the following sessions.

Asia: 5:00 am – 4:00 pm
Europe: 3:00 pm – 12:00 am
USA: 8:00 pm – 5:00 am

By looking at that, we can grasp the idea that the Forex sub-markets within a particular group of countries are active within those given timeframes. It means that if you are quite knowledgeable with how the market within the areas listed above, you can make some smart trading within those schedules.

Does that mean you can't trade within the other markets if you live outside a certain country or continent? You still can! What that time list simply implies is that the market of those groups of countries, which happen to be the biggest factors that play within the Forex world are most active during those respective times.

If you prefer a trading schedule in which the country where you live is not that active during a certain session, you can always trade for currencies in other countries that are active in your free time. Like what's mentioned earlier, the Forex market doesn't sleep technically. You can trade, buy, sell, and make profit 5 days a week, 24 hours a day, as long as you choose the right currency in almost any given time at all.

Difference Between the Forex Market and Stock Market

Aside from the fact that it's bigger than the Stock Market, Forex has no main office, in contrast to the former which has a main office for every country you can think of. If you heard about cryptocurrency which is also one of the biggest trading markets today, you may have heard about the term "decentralization."

Such a term means that there is no single person or business entity controlling the whole system. This is where the cryptocurrency business becomes very similar to the Forex market – which is defined by experts as a huge network of trading entities from practically everywhere in the world as long as a certain form of currency exists.

Those entities that comprise the said network are banks, private business firms, fund management companies, and even government institutions. As they merge together with their day-to-day operations, that is where the trading and profiting takes place.

Since those business entities vary in sizes and mode of operations, it's the main reason why currency values and prices rise and fall. If something goes wrong with the economy of a certain country, we can surely see that the price of its currency is affected too. Conversely, if the economy of another country goes so well, we could see its currency performing nicely too.

That is actually how Forex trading experts base their decisions from. Their speculations are based on what goes within the over-all business world of a country. If most of the big names in the commercial field are raking huge incomes, then that country as a whole should experience a great rise in its finances too.

Also, if the government of that country is actively doing business with other governments as well, like maybe if a political leader is buying petroleum or all sorts of fossil fuels from another country, then it should go without saying too, that the recipient government would experience some revenue spikes on its over-all economy.

When situations like that happen or fail to happen, that actually determines the rise and fall of the currency value. Since all countries are contributors to the overall structure of the Forex market, they are all important nodes or elements within the network mentioned. We can also say that the currency of a country is kind of like its "share" to the overall global market if we are to treat the Forex Market as a corporation.

Another major factor that contributes to the rise of a country's currency value is the employment rate that's taking place within it. If there are more jobs that are offered therein, it would mean that more people are working and are gaining some regular income. Furthermore, it will be very likely that workers from other countries will also be hired there, which would usher in currencies from the countries of those outsiders – trading and exchanging of money will rise significantly.

Now, I know you're thinking that there is a lot of information that you really need to grasp. Do you really need to understand all of it just to start trading? Not really. With just very small capital, and just a few hours of your time each day, you can already start trading. No hardships there.

However, if you wish to be a truly successful trader, you have to learn about the currency of the target countries that own the currencies you want to trade with. Itwould be a really huge deciding factor for your investment choices. The most successful businessmen are those that know their craft very well. You can't expect to be a good warrior if you don't know your weapons and the battle techniques of your enemy.

Of course, we won't be dealing with real villains within the Forex market, although you might encounter some really villainous people along the way as you hone your trading skills. The only enemy you'll ever face as a Forex trader is yourself, making bad decisions. We can then say that to beat the enemy, you need to make some very smart decisions, and to do that, we really need to have at least some basic understanding of how the economy works.

But if we think of it and summarize the tasks of a trader, all you need to understand is this, there are only 2 main actions that you will do: buying and selling. If you think that a currency is doing so well, then you buy it. If you think it's gonna go down, then you sell it. Think about the see-sawing analogy mentioned earlier. If you mix it up with your knowledge about the economy of a certain country, then you will always be on the good path of successful trading practices.

Knowing The Most Profitable Currencies

Like a good warrior who has good knowledge of his weapons and battle equipment, you who plan to be transformed into a wise Forex trader must know the basics of the most popular currencies that you can make a profit with. Currencies are named with some abbreviations. Let's iterate them one by one.

For the US we have the Dollar which has the symbol of "USD", also called "Buck"

For the European Union we have the Euro which has the symbol of "EUR", also called "Fiber"

For Japan we have Yen which has the symbol of "JPY", also called "Buck"

For the UK we have the pound which has the symbol of "GBP", also called "Cable"

For Switzerland we have the Swiss Franc which has the symbol of "CHF", also called "Buck"

For Canada we have the Canadian Dollar which has the symbol of "CAD", also called "Loonie"

For Australia we have the Australian Dollar which has the symbol of "AUD", also called "Aussie"

For New Zealand we have the New Zealand Dollar which has the symbol of "NZD", also called "Kiwi"

They are not the only currencies out there. However, most successful traders focus on these 8 major currencies because they are the most traded forms of money in the world. Looking at the given list would also give us the understanding that in connection to the "economy knowledge" stated above, there are also 8 countries that you need to really watch out for.

Such countries are the major key players within the Forex market so by default, being knowledgeable with all of them will surely give you the greatest advantage as a Forex trader.

Understanding Symbols Pairings

Let's understand what currency pairing actually means, and why they are paired in these ways:

EUR/USD

USD/JPY

GBP/USD

USD/CHF

USD/CAD

AUD/USD

NZD/USD

You might wonder why in the list above, the US Dollar appears in all items. It's because it has the most number of transactions going on in the world at all times. While the US might not be the ultimate richest country in the world, its currency has become the favorite single side of any Forex trading that ever exists.

When doing your actual trading acts, bear in mind that the position of USD is fixed and locked which means you can't really change it – Online platforms program their systems that way, for easier comprehension. If it appears on the left or on the right said of a certain pairing, you have to leave it as it is. Such a method makes the acts of trading much more simple for everyone especially for novice traders like you.

Exotic Pairs

When physical looks are focused on as a topic there is this thing called "exoticism." And although we're not talking about any outward beauty in Forex, we have to know that there is another kind of beauty going on within the market, and it is an exotic currency pairing at its finest.

Why exotic? Because they don't really belong to the "8 big leagues" in the Forex trading business. They are those that come from "not-so-popular-countries" in terms of currency power. Here they are with their corresponding symbols:

Currencies	Symbols
Euro – Turkish Lira EUR/TRY	:
US Dollar – Swedish Krona USD/SEK	:
US Dollar – Norwegian Krone USD/NOK	:
US Dollar – Danish Krone USD/DKK	:
US Dollar – South African Rand USD/ZAR	:
US Dollar – Hong Kong Dollar USD/HKD	:
US Dollar – Singapore Dollar USD/SGD	:

They are the most popular currency pairings within the "Exotic Category"

About Forex Quotes

To understand Forex pairs further, let's break down each part meticulously. Reading Forex quotes is one of the most fundamental things that an aspiring trader must learn, you have to know it this early. For this example, let's take a look at USD and Euro. As of this writing, the pairing of the 2 would give us a value of "1.1500" so it would give us this Forex Quote:

EUR/USD = 1.1500

That line simply means that if you invest on that pair, you'd get the amount stated by their equivalent numbers. So if you exchange your European money for American money, you'd have a total of 1 Dollar and 15 cents. The 2 components of that quote are actually labeled as "base currency" and "quote currency" – the one on the left side (EUR) is the base, while the one on the right (USD) is the quote.

To make it easier for traders to remember the respective values for each currency pair, the base currency is always assigned with the value of 1. As what's discussed earlier about trading as the act of buying and selling at the same time, we can say that a currency quote is what reminds you the amount you're dealing with.

So in the EUR/USD pair, you are actually selling Euro money while buying US Dollars at the same time. If you have it this way, USD/EUR, then you're actually selling USD money while buying Euro. Just bear in mind that the base currency, the one on the left, is what you'll be selling.

To make it simpler, we can write the formula this way:

EUR/USD : buy Euro, sell US Dollar

USD/EUR : buy US Dollar, sell Euro

The same applies to all currencies in existence. All you need to really understand and take note of is the symbol for each currency.

About Pips

What are pips? To simply put it, we can just say that "pips" is the plural form of pip. I'm just humoring you, don't get mad. As acronym that means "Percentage In Point," They are actually the rise and fall of the equivalent value of a currency pair. For instance. If you hear a statement that from a Forex trader that goes "My pairing is up by 1 pip!" it means that his EUR/USD transaction becomes 1.1501 from 1.500.

Likewise if you hear that trader say, "My pairing is down by a pip!" it means that his EUR/USD transaction becomes 1.1499. Counting pips is what determines your losses or winnings if you play the Game of Forex Thrones. The higher the pips are, the higher your income will be, the lower the pips go, the lower your profit will be. This is something that you should be good at if you wish to be truly profitable as a Forex trader.

Dealing With Brokers

In being a Forex trader, let's not forget one important entity: the broker. They are a group of people or maybe just one person that facilitates your money flow within the Foreign Exchange Market. If they are tasked to do one important thing, then they should get paid, right? So how much should we pay them?

Actually, they will just take a very little amount – very, very little. The transaction cost that the broker gets is actually called "spread." This term can also be referred to as the difference between the "buying price" and the "selling price."

For instance, if you frequently go to a bank or a money-changing firm, you would have most likely known that you are always shown with 2 price values: the value of the currency you're holding, and the one you'll be given once you go through with the exchange.

Now let's say the current buying price of Euro is 1.1511, and its selling price is 1.1513, then it means there is a 2-pip difference, that is then the amount the broker gets. Don't be too sad about it. Because it is just a very, very small amount considering that 0.1500 actually just means "15 cents."

So whenever you deal with the EUR/USD pair, and you buy them, you will be automatically subtracted with 2 pips, depending of course on the currency value at a given situation.

Pips In Relevance To Lots

We talk about Lots in the previous paragraphs. Now let's discuss them in relevance to Pips. We already understood that a Standard Lot is comprised of 100,000 units and has a volume of 1.00. Now that would give us a cost of Dollars per pip which is 10 Dollars. It means that it will be the multiplier that determines your profits or losses.

So if you have 100 Dollars it will be multiplied by 10, because it is the current price per pip.

So for instance, if the current Pip value moves to 20, then you'd have the total earnings of 200 Dollars. Likewise, if you lose, then you'd lose with the same amount, although actually, you just lose the original amount you staked during the initial trading process.

It goes to show that higher pips equate to higher wins, while it results as well in big losses too. Now if you're a bit scared about it, you can always switch to a Mini Lot, or to make it less scary, you can also choose Micro Lot, which is way smaller.

A mini lot has the equivalent of 1 Dollar which will give you a profit of 20 Dollars. A smaller win, but a smaller loss too. Micro Lot is 10 times smaller, which again, results in a much smaller win, and a much smaller loss. The math is pretty easy to grasp, right?

Understanding Candlestick Charts

"The world today communicates visually" – This is a statement that today's marketers and media creators can openly declare with zero-doubt indication. Whenever we see signages of all kinds, we now see drawings and symbols instead of words. In publications, magazines, books, and even their digital counterparts are so replete with diagrams and infographics that text and numbers are kept very minimal.

Undeniably, graphics and visuals are now becoming as important as words in making people understand something. With Forex trading, even though you will mostly deal with numbers, you will also deal with graphics a lot... illustrations that represent the rising and falling of monetary pricings from all over the world, graphics that are actually known to the trading world as candlestick charts.

Believed to have been popularized by Munehisa Homma, a Japanese rice trader during the 18th Century, it is now the basis used by traders all over the world in this digital age of ours. Even outside Forex, this kind of chart is also used in other fields such as cryptocurrency.

The candlestick chart is super-important for a Forex trader – it is the ultimate tool that one must use in order to come up with the best trading decisions. Trading is an art that can really make you rich, no doubt of that. But it isn't something that you can just put money into, and wait for it to pile up without really doing anything.

You really need to understand how money within the exchange market flows and to do that, you need to understand what a candlestick chart is, and how you can use it as a guide to embark on your trading adventures.

Candlestick charts are often regarded by some traders as more than just a trading tool that can read and predict prices. For them, those charts are also a means of behavior analysis – something that can make them them understand the possible outcome of market practices tomorrow, and in the next period of months, or even years.

Some experts even claim that candlestick charts are actually objects that can spell out human emotions because they tell us the buying and selling patterns made by people within the Forex market every day, and what could they be thinking as they go on about their transactions.

Before breaking down the elements of a candlestick chart, let's grasp a simple analogy from a rope-pulling game called "tug-of-war." Even if you haven't participated in that kind of game, you can certainly discern that it can be summed up by knowing which side pulls the hardest, and which side gets dragged over into the opposing side's domain.

When a tug-of-war battle begins, we can see that the 2 teams start at an even point: no winner, no loser. But as the battle ensues, we can then see that one team could be in greater power compared to others for a few seconds, but then would start to get overpowered by the other due to some underlying forces at play.

When the battle finally commences usually after just a few seconds, we can then see the true victor and the true loser. In Forex, that can then be declared as the closing of a trading day, or week. Bye then, you should be able to see if you've gained more, or lost more than what you have actually expected.

Such an analogy could be one of the best methods for understanding a Forex chart. When a particular currency is pulling a currency closer to its domain, it means that it is gaining higher value compared to the other currency it's paired with.

There are times when one team pulls strongly for a few seconds, but then gets easily trampled down as the opposing team unpredictably pulls back harder. In currency exchange, things can also be like that – unpredictable and erratic. But by gaining some experiences with charts constantly, you can somehow make productive predictions that can help you grow your money fast.

The Anatomy Of A Candlestick Chart

The very reason why it is named as such is actually due to a very obvious reason – it really does look like a candlestick, with protruding fuses on both ends. It has basically four parts:

High point – is the topmost part a Forex candlestick. It is kind of like the tip of the candle's string fuse.

Close point – the bottom of the high point line, or where the main body of the candle begins.

Open point – is the bottom of the candle's body, the tip of the low line.

Low point – the tip of the candle's bottom string fuse.

To have a clearer picture in your head of what a Forex candlestick looks like, we can say that it looks like a tube with short protruding strings on both ends. The candle's main body or the tube actually represents a trading duration. It could represent a single day, an hour, a day, an entire week, or even an entire month.

In the open point, it is where a trading day opens, and the corresponding price for a certain currency of that day. The "low point string" is the duration in which the currency at hand is at its lowest point. Conversely, the higher part of the candlestick is just the opposite of those.

Green candles are often referred to as "bullish candles" because well, they are raging like bulls in terms of making a currency attain a higher value.

Red ones are called "bearish candles" because traders think of them as slugging the value of your money like a slow-running bear.

When a candle is in full green, meaning it has no string fuses at all on either end, it means that it is a strong candle, representing a currency that performing extremely well. Conversely, a totally red candle with no thin lines at all means it's doing badly.

You have to note that when the candle's body appears red, it means that the value is lower than the expected lowest point, so it means that the currency is appearing really bad. We can think of it as the value becoming negative if we compare it to Algebra. Another way of saying it could be that a currency becomes lower than the original value when it was opened on a given day.

By looking at various candlesticks within a Forex market chart, we can then create our own analysis about the market's direction. It is then when we can make a smart decision about what particular currency to trade, and how long will we hold on to our money, and how soon should we let it go and trade it with something else.

Bear in mind that a good comprehension of candlestick charts is very fundamental to the success or failure of any Forex trading activity. When the direction of a chart is going up, it means that there are lots of currency buyers doing some purchases.

It means you should consider buying too because the value of that currency you're buying could be raised really high. It could be raised to a quarter, a half, or even many full times over... depending on trends and other factors.

When a candle is very short compared to its strings on its ends which are really long, and if that little candle is in the middle, it means indecision. It means that people find it hard to decide whether to sell or to buy currencies at a particular time.

Understanding Dojis

Let's understand another important set of symbols. A long vertical line with a very short horizontal line (the very shortened candle body) is called a "Doji" It means that the opening price of a currency is the same as the price when it got closed.

Dojis are actually shown as a typical plus sign, a plus sign with an extremely long vertical line, and a "T" with a rather long bottom. It is also called a "Dragonfly Doji."

There is also the "Gravestone Doji" which can be seen as an inverted T or the reverse of a Dragonfly Doji. When a candlestick looks like that, it means that the price of a currency opens and closes at the low point or very near it, and has a long topping tail. When a chart shows a Gravestone Doji, it would mean that trading at this point isn't a good thing. You have to wait for a while before the situation improves.

The lengthening and shortening of a candlestick could be due to people hearing about an economy or financial news, or a major event within a certain country's monetary status. It could also mean an increase or decrease in a country's tourism revenues.

But for a typical trader like you and me, the reasons could just be irrelevant. What we will just be focusing on is the simple fact that a currency's value is high enough and that we should take advantage of it.

There is also the "Spinning Top Doji" – one that looks like a plus sign but with a vertical line that becomes fat, very fat, and goes back to being thin again. From an emotional perspective of the currency buyers, there is almost no emotion depicted on the buying habits that are represented by spinning tops. It means that prices are not moving up or down significantly. It generally represents indecision to either buy currencies or sell them.

"When a real candle is long, it means it has the burning power to stay longer of course." The same is true with candlesticks in a chart. If the "wick of a candle" grows long, it means the value of the currency it represents is rising too. It also means that there are lots of emotions in it too – people are buying and selling efficiently within the real world which boosted a country's economy. Such kinds of candles are also referred to as "expanded range candles."

When looking at a chart as you formulate your analysis, one of the major factors you have to highly take note of is when a sudden lowering of prices happens. When it rises again higher than the previous high point, it is called a pullback, and it could be a sign that the currency can still rise higher.

Recurring pullbacks are actually beneficial to a long-term trading strategy because it represents a currency's consistent increase throughout a certain duration. Such a set of events within a Forex chart can just be regarded as a 3-point action, the rise of the value, the sudden lowering of it, and the rising which is way higher than the previous high point.

As long as you take notice of those 3, and if they are higher than the previous sets, then it means the currency is performing so well. By looking at the exact point of the pullback, you can think of it as your "support level." It means that you should hope that the next low point in the direction of the chart shouldn't go lower than that.

The opposite of that point is called the "resistance level." It is the next indicator that the next low shouldn't be lower than that too. If it does go lower than that, then the currency could be in a bad scenario. Another way of determining if the value is going desirably higher is that the current support level should be higher than the previous one, and so on and so forth.

If they continue to be displayed with that pattern, it means that the currency at hand is in an "uptrend," and that many traders are enjoying the benefits it gives. By consistently looking into that, you can really do some little tradings, or big tradings, depending on what your gut is telling you.

If you see that the current support level is lower than the one before it, then we have to expect that the currency is now on a downtrend, which means that there are more sellers than buyers.

The best way to deal with that gut feeling is to remember the "don't get greedy advice" from the previous pages. Little profits accumulated over time would result in big profits. It is so much better than expecting a big win but attain a big loss as well in just a single stroke.

Here's one crucial fact that you really need to bear in mind, no matter how good you become in analyzing candlestick charts, there is no guarantee that the analysis you can derive from them will always work at all times. Here's the truth about Forex charts, or any other trading chart for that matter: they're not really 100% accurate.

The rise and fall of those green and red candles are just representations of what could be possibly taking place, they're not actual-real time data that truly represent what's actually happening within the financial setting of a certain country.

While trading charts are created using the most sophisticated software and hardware technologies there are, they can't really predict human behavior and choices that are taking place in various global markets every hour or every day.

The most productive treasure-hunters don't just rely on a hunch or luck to locate and dig up buried treasure chests. They need maps and homing instruments to find what they're looking for. As a Forex trader, candlestick charts are your maps and compasses – treat them with the utmost importance, and success in trading will surely await you in the very near future.

Understanding the Market's Direction

It has been stated earlier in the discussion that becoming a successful Forex trader has something to do with understanding the international market flow. To achieve that, we can just stare at the 3 kinds of analysis that a Forex neophyte must just look into: fundamental, technical, and sentimental. What are they?

Fundamental analysis – This revolves around this simple idea: a bad economy means a decrease in currency value while a good economy is an increase in currency value. It would mean that you need to have some comprehension regarding a country's government debt, inflation rate, employment status, and other similar stuff. It's pretty heavy to grasp at first, but it's something that you really should have some high consideration of.

Technical analysis – The easiest way to deal with that is understanding Forex charts, which is something that we will discuss in the next chapters. There are basically 4 factors that comprise technical analysis: price action, supports and resistances, trends, and indicators.

Price action is simply about the rise and fall of the prices that correspond to each currency. Supports and resistances on the other hand represent the low and high levels of a currency that it is able to reach over time. Support gets manifested when a value drops to a point that should be the motivation for traders to buy some currency.

Trends will show the steady direction of a currency, often for prolonged periods. For instance, if a currency is going up steadily on its course, or if it drops in the same manner, they are called trends. Expert traders often use it to predict upcoming value changes within the Forex market.

Indicators are those points that tell exactly how high or how low a certain currency is. Seasoned traders consider them as tools that can help them with precise and specific trading decisions.

Sentimental Analysis – Are they things that can make you cry because of nostalgic past memories? No. they are actually sets of analyzed data regarding the positions of major players that participate within the Forex market. These are often the biggest banks and biggest business entities around the world. They are actually members of a huge group within the business world know as the Commitment of Traders.

Attaining Forex Expertise: Learning About Top Trading Strategies

Since you really want to be greatly successful in your dealings with currency exchange, you probably want to answer questions like:

How do the experts conduct their trading businesses?

What are their entrance and exit strategies?

How are they leveraging economic news and events?

How are they running their lives as they invest huge time and effort in their trading activities?

Those are questions that you really want clear answers for, so let's tackle them here. Let's get acquainted with crucial key points that truly define rich traders and poor traders. You can call them techniques or strategies, either way, is preferable. What matters is your absorption for each of them.

Strategy 1: Working On Your Attitude Towards Trading

Let's talk about habits. Are they crucial to the very essence of being a good Forex trader? Absolutely. Why so very few traders become rich and why plenty of Forex enthusiasts don't become wealthy is defined by this important factor called habit – because good traders make it their second nature to habitually trade for most of their daily routines.

While they may not do it each and every day of their lives, they do it a lot, obviously. Habits greatly matter in this discussion, so let's get right to it. Here are the traits that you need to learn:

Balancing patience and impatience

Can you patiently wait while being impatient at the same time? That sounds impossible. But the truth is, the big leagues of Forex have the 2 traits in a perfect balance. So what does it mean? In all of their trading acts, literally all of them, they get anxious and worry a lot all the time. They are quick to jump into whatever trading advantage they can see, but then, there are also times when they quickly get out of them too based on the chart trends they're seeing.

Although they can manage the levels of such feelings efficiently as they gain more experience, they really worry about how their day-to-day trading might eventually turn out – it is the chief reason why they always do their very best to come up with the best decisions.

While there are times when they are quick to get out from a strategy they're executing, there are a lot of moments too, in which they will just say "I will wait for a little longer to see how this move pans out." The best way to describe the patience/impatience trading balance is this: being patient with winning trades and being impatient with losing ones.

If we are to illustrate such a principle, we could think of it as a picture with a set of small red dots, and a single occurrence of a big green dot – red being an indicator of waiting, and green being a symbol for proceeding. Another set of small red dots, and another presence of a big green dot, the cycle goes on and on.

The bigger the dot, the bigger the move or monetary value that should be involved. And since red is represented as small objects, it means the action or value to be staked at those moments should not be very big too. If you understood that pretty well, and if you plan to make it a habit, then you should be on your way to becoming an excellent trader.

If you think that many of those great traders succeeded easily during their first tries, you'd be hugely wrong. In fact, most of them lose a lot more than you can possibly imagine. Even during their expert days, they still lose heavily. But what they do is they become impatient with their losses, that's why they are quick to come up with more solid plans and actions on how to improve on their methods.

Be impatient if you're learning less than you should, but be very patient on those things that you can't control – this a statement that should belong to your main driving force with Forex.

Focusing on higher profit instead of proving smartness

Everybody wants to prove they're brilliant, who doesn't? But sometimes, the smartest of us get too blinded by our own perception of ourselves in terms of knowing the right stuff to buy and invest on, that we fail to realize they don't get the highest returns of investment. No matter how wise or intelligent you are, you can't just implement your knowledge into how the Forex market works all the time because there are lots of people therein that are just way smarter than you.

You have to listen to what the market tells you, not the other way around. You cannot tell the market "Do this because my experience tells so," or "Do that because the knowledge I attained will prove me right." The market is what's right all the time, so listen to what it says.

You have to set your mind in choosing those actions that make the most money, not on how beautiful an investment object is, according to your own definition. So in Forex trading, you have to focus on the winning side always. Even if you dearly love a certain currency because of some nostalgic elements attached to it, you have to be quick to switch from one portion to another. Forget about currency loyalty. Instead, focus on one major aspect that can really make you succeed – your own money.

Using charts and visuals wisely

In the candlestick topic we discussed in the previous pages, it is emphasized that they should be absorbed and understood thoroughly because they are among the most useful tools in trading. Successful traders don't just look at charts, they internalize them deeply because aside from telling them the best directions the market is going, they can also tell where other good traders are lining up.

All traders perform technical analysis of some sort. It would be foolish to just trade without really thinking. While typical traders look at charts as nothing but bars and lines, rich traders look at them as pictures of other traders that line up as they move into or away from a certain buying act. They always picture in their mind that something is going to happen whenever they look at a particular behavior of a chart.

Before engaging in a certain trade, they identify the right spots to enter, but also look for a quick exit strategy, should something go wrong – that's one of the traits of successful traders. Novice traders are often too fast to get into a good trade because of too much excitement. Great traders don't think like that. If they can't tell where the exit points are in a chart, whether it's an increase or a decrease, they don't get in, it's power wisdom at play there. They gain big time by pointing out entrance and exit points clearly.

Learning from mistakes by moving on quickly

As you gain more trading experience, you might experience successive trades like 4 to 6 times that are so against what you hope for. Conversely, you might also encounter successive trades that go with you in a very positive way. This is natural. You have to absorb that in a statistical manner and accept that stuff like that could happen again and again.

When they do, you have to know that it's not because you are interpreting the market in the wrong way. It is simply because the market is just unpredictable at times that even the smartest analysts could end up very wrong too.

Although the importance of reading the charts right is emphasized in the previous item, you have to acknowledge that they don't work 100% of the time. Experts even claim that they just work 60% in most cases. Shocking and disappointing, right? But that's one of the realities that you just have to accept.

Another thing about big-time traders is that as long as there have been a series of wins with their past methods, those methods will prove in time that they will be effective again. They are not bothered by some of the losses they get as long as their previous statistics prove them to be profitable.

In dealing with the lows and disappointments of your previous trading, you have to think about those moments when the odds are in your favor. Learn from your mistakes but be quick to move on, there are better opportunities that ahead that await you.

Strategy 2: Choosing The Right Broker

Whenever you engage in any money-trading transaction in Forex, you need some kind of middle man. Not exactly a man, but an online business entity that will facilitate the transaction for you: From you Dollar to Euro, from Swiss Franc to Pound, from Peso to Yen, et cetera. Such a kind of entity that handles the changing of any of these currencies into another is called a "Broker."

Like any middle man in a real-world business setting, you need someone you can trust. After all, why would you entrust your hard-earned money to someone who has earned the reputation of swindling people's money away? While the money-making mechanisms that make Forex function is definitely not a scam, there will always be those that will use the very nice functions of the market as a scam.

Just like the statement in the Bible that goes "The love of money is the root of all evil," The problem is not money itself, but in the idea of how people deal with money and how they lie and cheat for the sake of attaining it. Forex, as a giant money-making system is also used by a lot of scammers and swindlers too, that's why it is really important that an aspiring Forex trader must know the proper steps in choosing the right broker.

In this section, let us talk about the proper guidelines and checklist in tapping into the right brokerage firms on the internet. Even experienced traders constantly look for truly trustworthy traders that might help them increase their profits even more. You as a newbie should do the same too since failure for you is never an option since you are someone who's super-excited to hit it big with Forex.

Traits of A Good Forex Broker

A good broker can be identified as having the following:

Looks for its own interests, but makes sure yours are looked upon too

Most brokers just want to gain profit from you but are not really interested in seeing you grow, and in witnessing you succeed with your trading endeavors. A good broker is someone who seeks really high gains but makes you tag along with it. Yes, all brokers are businessmen whose goals are to make money, and anyone who doesn't acknowledge this would be a fool. But a good broker would not just be focused on getting something from you, but also in getting something from the market, which he can then share with its clients, such as you.

If you remember the facts about Spreads in the previous sections, they are the amount that the broker earns by facilitating a trading act. Of course, all traders are doing the best they can to make the most out of their clients' Spreads, and you are of no exemption. But good traders attain their spreads in the fairest manner, they wouldn't be in the business for extended periods if they are bad at it.

Has excellent trading demos that anyone can openly view

Whenever we hear about the success of a businessman and wish to follow in the footsteps of that person, we would most likely see that person "walk the talk." A person who babbles about his success but has no concrete proof of it would be something that we annoyed listening to. To really know if your broker has the business prowess that can grow your money, you have to see for yourself if they have good trading demo videos that you can easily view and understand.

All legit brokers have their own websites of Youtube channels and in them, you should see some of their videos in which they perform video tutorials or live trading that you can take inspiration from or learn from. If you can see that their recorded videos produce almost exactly the same results as their live ones, then it is a surefire indicator that the broker you're considering to partner with has the business execution that can really make you rich.

It would be quite natural for brokers to upload videos in their channels about how they're better than their competitors. It is understandable that all businesses advertise their advantages and none of their disadvantages to all of their potential clients. However, it would be far better for you to focus on their demo and live videos more than on their advertising and promotional videos.

Many Forex brokerage firms will offer you trading courses for a certain fee giving you promises of doubling, tripling, or quadrupling your income. Some of these claims could just be an exaggeration, though some of them could also be very real as well. Tapping into such courses is fine, you should take advantage of them too if you're truly serious with your trading endeavors.

But bear in mind that there are free tutorials out there too. Sometimes, paying for training doesn't really pay off any better than the free ones. Some online course lovers highly prefer paid training with a coach instead of self-learning in which they just become lazy and sluggish.

Demo trading video streams are meant to show you the transition of the uploading and receiving of funds and you have to see if you can easily duplicate what the demonstrators do on screen. Pay for such skills or learn them on your own, the choice is yours.

Whatever works for you, just bear in mind that a good and successful trader doesn't rely on the decisions made by others. Although taking heed of the decisions of the best traders out there surely gives lots of advantages, the real advantage is having the skill to make decisions on your own. It will not only make your trading adventures so much emotionally rewarding, but more prolific as well in terms of self-growth and self-worth.

Has a wide selection of market options

One way to discern if a certain broker can be successful for the long haul is by looking at its selection of markets. The most-traded currencies are of course the Dollar and the Euro. But are they the only currencies out there? No. While they are truly the currencies that you can make the greatest money with, there will be times when other alternatives are also showing profit promises that could be truly rewarding.

If your broker has no easy way of changing other currencies that could just be minor key players within the entirety of the Forex market, it could be a huge indicator that they are not something that you should always work with. In the business world, opportunities come and go. Some of the best opportunities could arrive now, and be gone in a very short span of time.

In the Forex market, the rise and fall of money are really volatile. What's very high now could be very low in a matter of hours. What if you want to switch from one currency into another but your broker couldn't handle such a trading speed that suits your transaction preferences?

The best brokers should be instantly there whenever you want to immediately hop into a trading transaction that you want to hop into at nearly the speed of thought. While it's not really a beneficial habit when you constantly jump from one currency pairing to another, there are special times when you really need to, that's why it's super-important for a broker to be capable of handling speedy transactions especially if there are plenty of traders like us who wants to quickly attain the earnings we dream and wish for.

One of the trends in Forex trading nowadays is that Spreads are quite thin and small. Years ago, the fees that we need to pay to the brokers are quite high. But with the number of traders grown rapidly with each passing month, fees are getting smaller and more affordable, making anyone with very small capitals be able to participate in the games of trading.

This is a good opportunity for small-time individuals to increase their means of living. And all successful brokers do their very best to cater to even the smallest players who just want to start trading with their very small amounts. If a broker has a relatively high-rates of Spreads, you should avoid it because for sure, there will be lots of more affordable options out there.

The best way to find out who they are is to spend enough time practicing on your own account and connect with other new traders out there. Surely, there are plenty of individuals out there who are as non-educated as you in terms of Forex trading. You might think that you are Forex-ignorant, but there others out there who are more ignorant than you.

Do you know what's really cool? Many Forex broker experts don't care if your ignorant or not. They will surely have the means of helping you. Many of them are actually very friendly and helpful – it is one of the traits that make them very successful within the market.

If your chosen broker firm shows some unfriendliness, then then it is not the right one for you. Move on to the next ones on your list, some of them could be more worth your time.

Shows professional transparency

In dealing with friendships and partnerships in our social circles, we hate nothing more than those people who have hidden ulterior motives as they conduct those processes that they claim could benefit both parties: yours and theirs. Although they may sure do work hard in attaining some profit that can benefit both of you, knowing later on that your partner actually gains more than you could have without really explaining it to you would surely make you feel uncomfortable.

If your broker is showing such signs, then it is also an indicator that it is not a good brokerage firm. Even top-notch broker businesses in other areas that have very little thing to do with the Forex market are very clear with what they're doing. They don't show any signs of cheating on their clients are gaming the entire system just to their advantage.

Whenever you ask them questions, they will give you a straightforward answer as long as such answers don't breach their company's trade secrets. They are quick and swift in dealing with clients' queries and will waste no time in reaching out to us whenever we speak about troubles of any kind.

They are the kind of business firms that are very evident in their 2-way dealings. They are good at increasing their revenues, all the while showing great indications as well that their clients and partners as well are properly rewarded. They are the types of entities that make sure that it's a win-win situation between them and their prospective clients, inasmuch as in their dealings with the clients in the past.

Has excellent customer support

In connection to the "Forex never sleeps" adage, good brokers have customer service sections that never sleeps as well, and one that deals with problems in the quickest ways possible. While Forex isn't really 24-7, more likely being just 24-5 because it is closed during Saturdays and Sundays, the best broker firms have some staff that works even on those days, just to handle clients' inquiries and problems.

It doesn't mean though that those firms that are closed during weekends are bad ones. There are actually good brokers that are also closed during those days because the markets are also closed therein. However, when they do open, they are very quick and are highly reachable whenever you want to communicate with them through phone or through e-mail. Some of them even cater to video calls and teleconferences just to give the best possible services to their clients.

Has a wide range of trading tools

Aside from the excellent services and nice etiquette that they're capable of displaying, a good broker firm to pick would be one that has a wide variety of software tools that you can utilize to maximize your trading efforts. The best way to know this is by looking at the links and menus of their websites.

Are the links and link descriptions easy to grasp and comprehend? Are the sub-menus fast enough to access and learn from? Those are questions that you should find so easy to give answers to, by simply navigating through the interface of their web portal.

Since you already have some in-depth understanding of charts in the earliest chapters, you should also check if the broker's website has previous charts that you can check out and study – they will be excellent guides that can help you decide on your next trading moves.

Many popular broker firms have the habit of sending newsletters and press releases straight to your e-mail or social media accounts. Such methods are very cool strategies that can make their platforms even more attractive.

The online portal of a good Forex broker is something that should be a complete recipe on itself. Whenever you log on to their site, you have to be ushered into a set of tools, demo videos, and images that you can instantly use. They have to be so good and very comprehensive that you don't need other tools or supplements so you can understand the latest trends or methods better.

The Best Known Forex Brokers

XM – This is by far the most popular among beginners. Their most notable feature is their free $30 that you can use for your first trading experience.

IG – Globally speaking, this is the most trusted broker by most traders worldwide.

Saxo – If having a more in-depth knowledge about the Forex market is your goal, this should be your first choice.

CMC – This one shows you the widest options for currency pairs. This is where money connections can be found best.

Etoro – The best platform for those who wants to trade in the easiest way possible. Its main feature is "cop-trading."

Strategy 3: Mastering Your Own Demo Account

What's the next best thing to having a real dog? By having a stuffed-toy dog, or by having a figurine dog, that would be the safest answers to give. Of course, owning a dog is not really an extremely serious undertaking, unless you have the mind of an animal-rights activist. If you really know what it feels like to own a dog, why take an object that looks like a dog? Why not take a real, live dog that barks, wiggles its tail, and plays with you in your dull moments?

But here's the thing about real dogs: they will bite you, especially in situations when you will be harsh to them, or if you don't feed them enough. Now, what do dogs have in common with Forex trading? Well, nothing directly.

But if we're going to look closely enough, we might get to see that if you don't trade wisely enough, your Forex efforts will bite you, albeit painfully, because you will lose some precious earnings that should have been better investments somewhere else. That's where Forex and dogs are a bit similar. – Lame analogy, but one that you have to contemplate on.

Using A Forex Demo Account: The First Crucial Step To Take

Now, let's get a bit more topic-centered. How can you be truly well-versed in the very acts of trading? Should you invest real money on a real trading act right on? What if you'll lose? What if you'd gain regret instead of more motivation to proceed with your endeavors as a successful Forex investor? Fret not and fear never, because most Forex brokers offer something that all trading newbies would be very pleased with: demo accounts.

With such an account, you will be granted access to an online portal in which you can conduct some trading practice using digital money that represents your first trading amounts. All you need to key in are some numbers like your supposed dollar deposit, the currency pairing of your choice, your entry point, and your exit point. You will be then prompted to begin the trading simulation which actually looks and feels like it's a real trading activity.

By doing it again, and again, you will surely begin to understand the ins and outs of a trader's life. Which will gradually transform your mode of thinking. Demo accounts are free and are easy to acquire. It just usually involves the following:

- having an email account
- having a computer or smartphone that you can regularly use
- choosing the right broker
- logging on to your chosen broker's website and signing up
- waiting for a confirmation email
- downloading their trading interface and installing it to your phone or computer
- configuring your trading settings and starting the actual trading

Performing all of these steps may vary a little depending on your chosen broker's platform. But they basically work the same. There is no need to worry about not learning how to start, as their menus and guides are very comprehensive.

Choosing the best trading practice platforms is also very simple. All it needs is just the proper keywords in Google's search bar. To make it even easier for you, you can just simply go to Forex.com where you will be guided easily to your first trading experiences. In case you want to have a feel of social trading, going to Etoro.com would also be a very wise choice.

What is the importance of practicing using a demo account?

Because jumping right into real trading using real money is often emotionally painstaking, using unreal money that simulates real trading scenarios would be very ideal for a Forex beginner. You can begin trading right away, experience failure, and then restart the activity again and again. As you get into the habit, you will attain some considerable wisdom along the way and will be having lesser levels of fear whenever you decide to conduct real trading acts in the future.

But like an aspiring boxer fighting punching bags and sparring partners in the gym, using demo accounts has some disadvantages as well. Let's talk about them so you'll have better insights into the act.

Brokers may intentionally let you win more

Forex brokers are businessmen who want to attain more clients. And in order to do so, they will surely do their very best to make their platforms very attractive. Since that is the goal, they will most likely show that within their domain, you will surely win most of the time. Although expert traders will easily spot that, you as a novice will not see that through easily, as you are someone who really wants to get rich quick.

Although what happens in a real trading act is what's depicted in a demo account simulation, it's just exactly what it is: a simulation, unreal, fake, an imitation. The psychology behind the deed is there, but the actual learning gain is much lower.

You might get encouraged to overtrade

"Too much of a good thing is actually bad." – This is a very famous adage. Even in Forex trading, the same principle applies. Ask any experienced trader, and he or she will most definitely tell you: "Don't overtrade my friend, it does more harm than good." If doing the same thing again and again can make you better and wiser, wouldn't overtrading make you a better trader? No. Becoming a good trader is built on trading at the right time with the right mindset. Much like the idea that "The best sex is not due to oversex."

If you eat a top-class pizza delicacy, it will be very tasty during the first few slices. But eat an entire jumbo order by yourself, and you'll be sick physically and mentally as well. If you're forced to commit such an act, multiple times, the resulting outcome would be severe vomiting and withdrawals. You will then have it in your head to avoid eating pizza for the next years to come.

Of course, trading is different from eating. Experts have this to say: "Overtrading will make you see things in charts that aren't really there, and will let you make foolish decisions." Bear in mind that gamblers in casinos really can win, but most of them lose because they don't know when to stop or when to take a rest.

To be truly efficient in Forex, never overtrade. And in spending too much time with demo accounts, you just might fall into that trap. Avoid it at all costs.

You might not get the proper psycho-emotional learning.

Forex trading is an emotional undertaking – that's something that you should highly put in mind. Why many businessmen become so successful is they don't only invest time and money in their endeavors, but emotions and mental efforts as well. They formulate plans, review them methodically, and put those plans to work. How those plans get changed or executed differently will be based on what people feel or how they may react to the products they bring out into the world.

Because you're not actually dealing with real money, you won't be expecting real failure should anything go wrong. For that, you will be less scared, which makes you hop into false bravery, which will eventually push you into making wrong decisions.

But before you become too discouraged in signing up for a Forex demo account, you should take heed of this declaration: the advantages of demo accounts far outweigh the disadvantages. Here's why.

They will teach you better than tutorials and articles can.

There are tons of videos and articles that serve as Forex trading guides all over the internet. Many of them are actually very helpful resources that can really make you an expert in the shortest time possible. But as what's stated earlier, experience is still the best teacher. Although watching those videos and reading those articles can surely help you get into the vibe, nothing feels better than being on an actual trading exercise. It is the only way of truly illustrating from a mental standpoint what the action is really all about.

They will show you the realities of the daily life of a trader, minus the financial expense.

Successful trading is a way of life, and you can't be rich with it if you don't make it your second nature, or at list within the list of your regular "to-do list." But making trading as a way of life would be very expensive money-wise for a beginner like you. Demo-trading is the cheapest and most accessible way of replicating the daily dealings of an expert trader and for the time being, no better option is there yet.

Those are only 2 advantages, but their weight should be understandably heavier than the disadvantages. Start your own Forex demo account right now so that the expertise you're hoping for will only be a few steps away from you.

Strategy 4: Using The Scalping Method – The Key to Attaining $10,000 a Month

If you truly believe that "slow and steady wins the race," then you have to highly consider learning the most effective trading strategy yet: Scalping. Before we begin discussing this technique, you have to go back into the topic "The Trading Tasks That A Forex Newbie Must Undergo," so you'll be refreshed with the technicalities that this discussion will show you.

So what is scalping? As the root word suggests, it is a technique in which you will scrape some earnings little by little, usually just a small percentage of the capital you're trading. Most traders who are fond of using it has a 10% rule – They make it a habit to put in 10% of their capital, make a trade, take the 10% increase of their profit, and get out. They do it 9 more times and by adding all of the profits, they would then evaluate and calculate if they got the winnings they hope for.

Some trading experts say that the risks involved with scalping are very high, while some view it as a means of attaining the best stream of income because the rewards are quite high too. Whenever you consider applying this technique to yourself, you should weigh it carefully from your own perspective.

But many traders are getting some decent success with it, that's why you should give it time to try it out to see if it works for you. For the next few pages, you will be ushered into the one of the best keypoints promised in this book: *how to attain a 10,000-dollar income each month.*

Steps to take in using scalping

Observing pivot points – Knowing exactly where a currency begins to drop or where it starts to rise is highly important, that's one of the key factors that make many Forex investors successful. There is no definitive way of predicting when exactly a pivot point happens. However, understanding the highs and lows for the previous days is really helpful in making a good trading decision.

A pivot point can be viewed as an indicator coined by floor traders so it will be much easier to determine possible turning points of whether a certain price will go up or go down. By understanding pivot points, you can easily detect if the market's sentiment can go from bullish to bearish – bullish meaning green candlesticks and bearish meaning red.

They are the means of determining the exact "support and resistance levels," of a chart. We will have to draw lines in the chart the levels of the rise and fall of the market so we can know exactly when to get in and when to get out.

Observing yesterday's chart movements – This is also important so we can have the idea of the market's direction for the present day, and in the next days. Because 2 of the elements that make Forex function is tourism and product exporting/importing, they are among the chief reasons why charts show some rising and falling of currencies. And the thing about such events is that most of them happen for days, which means that yesterday's trend could just be the same today.

Since we understood already that pips determine our profit, knowing the average pips of yesterday's charts would be a good move to choose. For instance, if you entered a trading act using a currency pair that's equivalent to "1.6400" and it can be seen that most of the pips during the previous days are around 50 to 75 (that's today's common range for the EUR/USD pair), it would mean that you'd get an estimated earning of "1.6450"

You have to take into account that the value of a pip can be calculated this way: 1 divided by 10,000. That would give us an exchange rate of 0.0001. Remember, 50 to 75 pips are just the typical rise or fall of candlestick movements; they are not always exact not accurate, that's why it is essential to observe yesterday's chart movements. If you've clearly understood yesterday's chart visuals, it should be safe to do some scalping trading for today.

Scalping is actually done as a series since we will just be scraping little earnings and gathering them altogether to assess our winnings. For that, it would be wise to have a money management strategy as you get on with it.

Money Management With Scalping

For this example, let's work with a capital of $100 for a beginner, that is not a small amount. But let's just use the number for now so the Mathematics behind our following analogies would be a bit easier to follow. And also, it would be profitable for you anyway, as long as you already got the logistics right. Bear in mind that small capitals will also result in small profits.

If you want to take some considerably high profit as a beginner, it would be good to start with a hundred bucks. Now, in using scalping with that amount, let's say we engage in a trading series comprised of 10 trading moves. For each move, we will put in 10 bucks so we can attain that 10% rule which should be the goal too.

The ultimate objective of scalping is to attain a tenth of our capital each time, to maximize our winning trading potential. Just think of this strategy as making a 10% risk, which should also result in an estimated 10% result of profit.

For this example, let us use the EUR/USD pair as they are obviously the most popular currency pairing in existence. Let us set the number "5" as our "take profit" point and "50" as our "stop-loss" point. This means that once our earnings have equaled 5 pips, we should already take that as a win, and take our earnings already. If we see that the pips have gone down to 50 pips, then it would be time to stop since we are apparently losing.

You might begin to think that if our possible win is just 5 points and our possible loss is based at 50, does it mean that we will lose more than we could win? Actually, we shouldn't view it as such. Why we set 5 as already a win is because it is a good amount already. If we wait for it to rise higher, we could lose – it is a good practice to take the win even though it's just a small one. By habitually doing that, your "little earnings" will pile up and become "big earnings in the long run."

About that 50-point stop loss, it means that even though the values are getting lower, it means that we're not giving up just yet. It implies we need to wait for a while because the values could rise higher in the next moments. If it goes lower than 50 though, it would be wise to call it day and wait for greener opportunities in our next trading sessions.

Understanding the effectiveness of scalping

The success rate of this technique, according to the experts themselves, is 90%, which means that for a series of 10 trades you will do with scalping, you could lose only once… provided or course that you have studied and understood the charts of yesterday clearly. Experts claim that 90 is just the safest margin. They declare that if you mix up your endeavor with excellent technical analysis, your success rate could be much higher.

Some seasoned traders can attest that with scalping, you can already attain a success rate that high within an hour if you get lucky. But if you have more time to spare, it would be nice to not make it too short, just to keep it safe.

If you remembered the previous pages' recommendation of the XM Broker as an ideal choice for beginners, it would be best to use the company for scalping because they have this Ultra-Low Spread Account that could be as low as 0.6 spreads.

In case you missed what a spread means, it is that amount that you will pay to a broker like XM, who facilitates a trading transaction within Forex. By choosing a broker with a low spread, it is a means of maximizing your possible earnings.

In starting the actual scalping method, the presence of another account which should serve as your "storage account" is recommended. Inside it will be that a hundred bucks we mentioned earlier and the other account will be the recipient of the ten bucks that will hold the amount that we will use for each element of our trading activity.

In trading, there is this term called "slippage" – a term that describes those damages or wasted portions of our earnings. This can be viewed as those little droplets of the drinks we're sipping during mealtime or those little grains of rice that got lost during transport if we are a rice trader. Such a scenario is natural. It would be unwise to fail to recognize it.

So to prevent your main account from suffering some damages, it would be wise to deposit an amount into another account so that our main account will not be affected. Once you deposited the $10 already, we can then begin trading.

The Math behind scalping can be easily understood by just looking at the first few wins of your trading series. For instance, if in your first trade, you have a $1 win, your total earnings have just reached $11 as it gets added to your initial capital of ten bucks. If you stake it again for the next trade, it could grow by 10% each time.

Now if you execute the same process 10 times in a row, provided that you win each time, you'd accumulate a total amount of $115.939, that is after you've completed the entire series of 10 trades. Once you've done that. It would be good to withdraw your earnings, and stake in another 10 bucks for your next series of trades. You repeat the same process, again, and again.

But does this technique always makes you win? No. like what you've been told in the previous pages, there is no exact way of accurately predicting chart movements and market direction at a 100% rate. For this reason, experts suggest that if you've experienced 2 losses or more losses with scalping, you should stop trading for a moment.

Let's get back to your goal: Accumulating $10,000 a month. Is that a realistic goal? It is, if we adhere to 3 solid approaches: 1.) a realistic mathematical formula, 2.) a realistic perspective on how many trades you can make for a month, and 3.) a much bigger capital. Experts claim that for each single day, you can only make 5 effective and reasonable trades. And since there are only 20 business days in a month, it means it would be unwise to exceed 100 trades for that duration.

If we are to accept that, then it also means that having a $100 capital is not enough. If we increase it into $110, it means we could attain an estimated total earnings of $127.53 for 10 trades. And going back to that ideal 100 trades per month, it means we can accumulate a total of $12,753. Seems good, right?

But we have to remember that there's no guarantee that you'd have 10 straight wins, let's just say that the 2,000 is the slippage we mentioned earlier. We might say that it is our "margin of error." Remember, no strategy, no matter how smartly crafted is ever perfect.

Bear in mind, don't overtrade. You must constantly remind yourself that greedy traders don't get too far in the trading business. When there are times that you're experiencing some losses, it means that the currency pair you're focusing on could be in a bad situation. In that case, give it a rest and pick another good time to trade. Take some time to analyze what went wrong with your previous efforts so you can formulate better plans and better strategies in the future.

Best Methods of Making Forex So Much Easier

While getting through the previous discussions, you might have this notion that "Forex trading has a lot of deep analysis requirements that you need to get by." Hate the idea for what it truly is, but that's just a reality for a market trader. You can't get rich with the art of trading without getting through the mental processing needed to be successful at it.

But is Forex really that difficult? Must a novice trading enthusiast really have to go through all the seemingly unbearable difficulties mentioned earlier? With all seriousness, all expert traders will really say yes. That's just the best way to answer it.

But what if you want to take the easy way? Isn't there a much more convenient set of methods that can give you profit with Forex without experiencing extreme hardships? Thankfully for you, and for all those Forex aspirants who want to take the easy path, a comprehensive guide awaits you. Keep reading.

Engaging in copy-trading

Because Forex has been around for nearly 50 years already, many successful individuals are already very well-versed at it. As such, many of them are so good at what they do that failure is almost an impossibility whenever they conduct trading acts on any given day of their profitable lives. In that case, wouldn't it be best for the enthusiasts to mimic what they're exactly doing?

The best approach for that would be to study what they're doing: read writings about them, or watch videos of them as they perform such actions. After having some comprehension, we would then take some actions based on what we've learned. Amazingly though, that's not what copy-trading is all about – it's actually employing an automated system that imitates exactly what those expert traders are actually doing.

To simplify it further, we're talking about a computerized procedure that will facilitate the linking of your account with that of the trader whose actions you want to copy. Whatever are the outcomes of that person's choices and decisions, so will be the outcome of your account.

But there is actually a catch with that technique. By doing copy-trading, a small portion of our profit will be directed to that trader you're linked with. You are benefiting from his actions, it would be unfair for you to just take profits without paying anything to the one who does all the action. It just seems justifiable for the system to work that way.

Copy-trading is closely related to mirror-trading. It works basically as something that would pop into your mind if you'd think about mirroring. It means that that the actions that will happen within your account is a duplicate of someone else's. Both copy trading and mirror trading are components of a system called "social trading" – a system that takes advantage of the network of traders that are actively participating in the Forex world.

With the accumulated knowledge gathered from the network, any Forex aspirant can greatly benefit from tapping into an array of benefits. It started as a trend in 2005 and since then, it has been a favorite thing for aspiring traders. The fact that people are attaining some success with it should make us think that it must have some reasons that make it so attractive:

Advantages of copy-trading

- There is very little effort that you need to pour into it.
- You just set the amount you want to trade, and wait for the expert trader you're copying to make a profit for both of you.
- You are gaining earnings with trading, but are also able to do your daily chores in life

But you have to take heed to the following too.

Disadvantages of copy-trading

- It has lesser returns of investment
- An expert trader's failure will be your failure too (Yes, they fail at times too, though such failures are

dependent on their reputation so you can just look them up and make your decision of copying them.)
- You will learn very little with actual trading, which means becoming an expert is something you'll never be.

If you want to hop into the ease and comfort that copy-trading can offer, here are 2 good platforms you should check out:

Etoro – A trading company established in Israel. Founded in 2007, it has been one of the most profitable firms in the field of trading having accumulated an estimated total value of $800 within its 2-decade operation. Israel is a country known for its successful startups and sophisticated technological breakthroughs, which makes it easier for us to put our trust in Etoro.

Zulutrade – Also founded in the same year as Etoro, it is a Greek-managed company that's declared by Daily Telegraph as one of "The Best 100 Startups" in the category of Finance and E-commerce. One of its most notable features is ZuluGuard, a system that automatically you to unfollow a certain trading act if something changes with the acts of the trader you're copying.

So mirror-trading and copy-trading work basically the same. What is the notable difference between the 2? The simplest answer to the question would be this: That the former is better suited for those who want to have bigger volumes of profit, while the latter is more applicable for those who want to have smaller incomes.

Mirroring works best with higher capitals because it is often related to major trading entities. Copy-trading works within the framework of one individual trader to another. This can give us the understanding that it is most suited for small trading investments. So as a beginner and as someone who has only a small amount at your disposal, copy-trading might just be the best option for you.

Does copy-trading really work? Yes, it really does. In fact, most experts have the estimate of a 10% profit that one can attain yearly, which shouldn't be so bad for someone who doesn't want to invest on a huge amount of time with trading on a daily basis.

Working with trading coaches and consultants

Because Forex trading is a very serious undertaking indeed, you might want to consider seeking professional help in attaining success with it. As such, tapping into the wisdom that trading coaches and consultants can give shouldn't be a bad idea. They have been trading consistently for years which means that their experiences have given them concrete methods already that can make anyone learn quickly and easily.

When choosing consultants, you will surely meet people who make exaggerated claims. That should be something you have to consider as something that's natural. Not all of them are all promises though. Some of them actually have the skills to truly deliver, and some of them can actually make your dreams come true.

But how do you find the best Forex trading consultant? While finding the best is not really easy, and not to mention expensive, choosing a good consultant might be something that's attainable and more realistic.

Here are the best traits that you should look for in a good trading consultant or coach:

1. **One that has been in the business for years already** – Sure, longer doesn't always mean better. But let's not forget that experience is the best teacher. One who else to look for a good teacher than someone who has been doing the act for longer periods already? A good Forex coach has to be a trader who has been to a series of ups and downs already. It is the only means by which he can give you the best indications of when to proceed, and when to halt or back down.

2. **One that you can communicate with easily** – In every relationship, communication is a very vital key. Without it, any undertaking would collapse before it even starts. In planning to hire a consultant, be very sure that he or she is very reachable and accessible.

One of the best ways of figuring this out is knowing if the consultancy services being offered has a website or social media page that you can easily exchange messages with. Also, be very sure that the consultant in question is available for video calls because seeing the face behind the business transaction is something that should be highly considered.

3. **One who has a great understanding of your goals** – The most successful trading coaches are the ones with the greatest understanding of how to attain the goals of the business. But what about your personal goal? Do you have the indication that the consultant you're planning to hire completely understands your own objectives? If that coach often talks about his own success but can't clearly give details about how the 2 of you might achieve your goals, avoid that person, he will not be worth your time and investment.

How much would consultancy cost you? It's hard to come up with an accurate answer. But the safest bet would be that it would surely fall within the 10% fraction of your earnings. Ten is actually that magic number that works so well in any digital-information dissemination. For instance, it can be observed that for every internet promotion of a product, nearly around 100 people will respond to every group of 1000 people reached.

It means that even though a product ad will show up to a person's wall news feed, only 1 for every 10 of those ads will be checked out by that person. The response rate could be higher or lower, depending on the beauty or usefulness of the product therein. Given that fact, it would be safe to say that consultants and coaches will never take a commission that's equal or higher to 10% of your earnings.

With online courses and webinars, the figure could be much different. For a certain payment, you could enroll in some kind of training where you can understand the ins and outs of trading, which you can employ to your advantage whenever you decide to embark on your first trading adventures.

Here's the plain and simple truth, hiring professional consultants or coaches is actually expensive. As a beginner, it would be best to just connect to a trader within your social circle. By choosing someone who's just within your arm's length reach, you can get the wisdom you need, provided of course that the person does not belong to the "douchey, a-hole category." Choosing this action would be very low-cost on your part as it would just be a "friendly partnership" of some sort.

What if you have nobody in your social circle who's into trading? You can find an endless sea of people who are very much on the same page as you, and they can be within reach via Youtube, Facebook, LinkedIn, or any social media website you can think of. Surely, there are lots of pages and online communities out there that you can tap into.

Join them, communicate with them, reach out to them. You can find countless like-minded individuals who can guide you and motivate you into taking huge undertakings within the Forex world. You can also just self-educate yourself, there are countless video tutorials out there that you can binge-watch anytime at your convenience.

Employing Trading Robots

We live in a generation that's replete with computers and a bunch of other digital things. Without a doubt, their existence has automated a lot of processes. What's so time-consuming in the past can now be done in a matter of minutes or even seconds.

How cool would it be to just utilize the presence of computers and the software inside them to do the trading for us, instead of ourselves staring at screen displays so we can come up with the analysis needed to make money? It is very cool of course. Do you know what's even cooler? Is that there are actually Forex Bots that you can employ to make trading even a lot easier.

What is a Forex Bot? It is a computer program employed by some brokers that automates trading decisions based on typical patterns generated by currency charts. Powered by Artificial Intelligence, it is designed to remove people's burdens of the psychological aspect of trading. Like real physical robots making heavy jobs in factories a lot lighter, these software bots are also helping beginning traders enjoy their trading acts greatly.

How does a trading bot work? The concept of its operations can be understood with a trader's habits and patterns being keyed into a certain bot's interface. It could also happen by letting the bot run along with a particular trading act. Once the bot's AI already figures out a certain trader's strategy, it will then create an automated procedure that can be executed without intervention.

All a trader needs to do is configure some commands and numbers, and the bot will perform its task, raking in some income as it does so tirelessly and relentlessly, even while the investor is sleeping, or doing whatever chore he can get his hands on. Brilliant and convenient, right?

What are the best Forex Bots? There are so many automated bot traders out there that declaring who's the best will be very hard for even the best analysts. The following are the ones worth checking out. They are listed along with their corresponding deposit rates:

Bot Name:	Minimum Deposit:
GPS Forex Bot 3	$100
Forex Trendy	$250
X Trade Premium	$100
Cento Bot	$250
Walls Street Forex Bot	$1,000
Forex Diamond	$1,000
Forex Gump	$4,000 on a
regular	account,

$400 on a nano
    account

What's up with those deposit rates? They actually
speak for the effectiveness of those bots that
correspond to each of them. Basically, the higher the
price, the higher the chance of earning big. To know
the success rates for each of them, it would be good
to Google them up for a better understanding.

Do Forex bots really work? Because they are systems
built by experienced traders and really smart people,
they really do. Many Forex popularizers are actually
gaining big profits out of their acts of selling Forex
bots. The existence of lazy money-rakers is
undeniable, and many software developers and Forex
businessmen are exploiting such a fact.

But here's something that you should really put in
mind: The best racers never rely on the auto-gear
features of even the best cars. While very good cars
can really spell the difference between an excellent
racer and a mediocre one, which makes world-class
racers the best of their kinds are their skills and wits.
They don't use auto-gear, that's just a solid fact.

To sum all of this up, you have to engrave this in
your mind: copy-trading, mirror-trading, and trading
bots, can really help you, and they can make your
Forex undertakings so much easier. But they're the
type of techniques that you can use if you just want
to make trading as a side-hustle. Think of them as
little tools that can augment your earnings.

But If you really want to get serious with Forex trading, never rely on the presence of anything that can automate the process for you. They're great tools to learn from, and they can really do the work if you don't have the time for some actual trading. But if you're in it for the long haul, or if you want to hit it big, learn from real experiences and from real people – there is no substitute for the golden knowledge and wisdom that you can attain from them.

How to Get The Right News for Best Investment and Make Money Online

When you get a stream of wins with Forex, the most likely thing to happen is that you'll be adding the habit of trading as a very important part of your daily routines in life. If it brought you massive amounts of income, would you ditch the habit? Definitely not. You will be trading some more tomorrow, and for the next years to come. That will be an infallible prediction that is if… you have made some success out of currency trading.

But as what you have truly understood by now, all global financial markets that use Forex as the main driving force changes a lot dramatically from time to time. By acknowledging that fact, we have to also embrace the idea that being many steps ahead among other traders is one of the key elements that will make us remain successful in the field of trading.

Knowing this, it is quite clear that we have to learn some skills in getting the right news to come up with better investment decisions.

Here are 2 tips on how you might be able to achieve it:

1. Knowing about how the employment system works

The employee-to-employer scheme of things play a very crucial role in the entirety of the realm of Forex, let's not forget about that. This means that we have to pay attention to it too if we plan to be truly serious with our trading endeavors in the future.

In connection to the previous item, we really need to have some solid idea about the flow of financing on a global scale. It's really hard to make predictions about this but to play it safe, it would be wise to be at least be advanced for "half a year to 18 months." There is statistical data that supports such a claim. For instance, most young people, who comprise a great majority of the workforce in nearly all companies in the world today usually hop from 1 workplace to another in a span of that duration.

We have to acknowledge that many young professionals rarely stay at their jobs for 2 years. 18 months should be a fair assessment as an average. Given that, we should consider accepting that the economy can really change within that span of time.

So in your trading activities in the next months or in the next few years, studying how the employment system works should be a wise investment of your time as well. For sure, you can come up with a much deeper analysis and speculations about how currency prices could rise or fall.

The world is virtually smaller now because of the existence of telecommunication along with the presence of high-speed planes and ships. In this era where the concept of "work from home" is becoming extremely popular, its effect on currency exchange could be really vital for the over-all scenery of the global economy. That's something that you really have to watch out for.

2. Advanced understanding of the status of the Euro and the US Dollar

There is no argument needed about the supremacy of the EUR/USD pairing. Since they are so relevant today, it is very unlikely that they will become quickly irrelevant for the next few years, or even decades. The very smart traders of today always look into these 2 currencies closely, as an Eagle would on its prey, as a high-definition camera would to an object being shot at. To be very good at such efforts, it would be truly wise to look at the economical flows of the countries within those financially bustling areas. It would be a huge mistake in choosing not to.

You may find it a bit trivial, but some expert traders take hold of information that isn't directly related to daily dealings with Forex. For instance, some traders absorb the idea that the physical design of the US Dollar Bill hasn't changed since 1929. To simply put it, existing paper bills that come from that era are still usable today. So if your grandpa has some treasure chest buried somewhere with some dollar bills in it, you could still use it now. Seriously.

Such a fact could make us discern more about the significance of the US Dollar. If you add it up with some daily small doses of what's happening within the economy and government settings of the Americans, you should be on the right path of a much broader understanding of Foreign Exchange. Consequently, better trading decisions from your head will just get channeled outwards, as you conduct more trading transactions each day.

Also, poking closely into the financial flows and events that traverse among the countries near England would be helpful too. The reason why the Euro is a much stronger force than the US Dollar is mainly due to this one simple truth: the economy is much more stable there, and that there are significantly richer business entities in Europe altogether, compared to those that are in the United States.

Although many US-based companies are also existent somewhere else, they will still be a minority compared to the vastness of the sea or mega-rich entities across Europe. By understanding the economies of the governments there, as well as the "money-funnels" that thrive within the area, you can have a good understanding of where the Euro will go in the next years or decades.

Now let's talk about ideas that can help you earn some additional income online.

5 Ways of Making Money With Your Forex Knowledge Online

Let's say you've been into trading for quite some time, and have been gaining some wins with most of your trading gigs. You've been pretty successful and are starting to have some considerable augmentation of your income. What do you do? Keep on trading without sharing your knowledge? No, because you as a noble person are somehow under the realization that such a kind of thinking would be an unkind trait to have.

Even if you're not considering it, let me encourage you that imparting your trading skills and learnings would be a cool thing to do, because it would not only make you earn more, but could also make you a hero to others. If there are ways that you knew about but are not sharing them to people who might need them, wouldn't that be selfish?

"But I don't want to be a hero!" you might blurt out. Yeah, perhaps. But what about the fact that you can make some extra earnings with some techniques that aren't directly connected to the very acts of trading, wouldn't that be some sort of amazing accomplishment?

Before the argument gets too long, let's just get right to it. Here are some ways in which you can make profit with your knowledge about Forex trading:

By publishing your writings on the web

For this option, blogging would be a very good first choice. A great bulk of the internet websites that exist today is mostly a pile of blogs. If they are that plentiful, then it means many writers are exploiting the very idea of publishing their knowledge and experiences every day, while making great piles of income along the way.

Take note, many of these bloggers are actually just plain, household individuals. They're not even the kind of people who were able to attain degrees in journalism or those who attended a series of writing workshops. They're just people who are into the habit of writing regularly and consistently.

The cool thing about article-publishing on the internet today is that people don't really care if you're a good wordsmith or not. All you have to be is someone who can put your ideas into writing in a simple-enough manner that they can figure out what you're trying to say in a "street-level approach."

As long as you can just explain your ideas into a form of writeups that would be simple enough for an elementary-grader, you are already a profitable blogger in the making. To make the idea simpler, learning about the likes of WordPress, Wix, and Blogspot would be a good start.

In terms of hosting your blogs within a webserver, Googling up Godaddy or Hostinger would be a great way to start your journey. You need not worry about how to actually start, as there are countless tutorials on the web that you can use to self-educate yourself. It shouldn't be that difficult for a novice, aspiring blogger like you.

How much can a blogger possibly earn? Novice bloggers, or those that we can categorize as writers who have been blogging for a year mostly claim to earn around $200 a month, and that's just a side income.

For those who blog seriously for 2 years or so, many of them claim to earn around $800 to $1000 a month. And again, that level of income is just for the average blogger. What if you become a well-loved blogger who discusses about Forex? You could earn a lot higher!

Another option you might want to choose is by publishing ebooks. They might not be as expensive as real books but that's basically the point. Because ebooks are cheaper, they're more affordable from people's perspectives, which make them very attractive kinds of stuff to buy. Should you hop into this method, selling your Forex ebook at $5 per download would be a good price level for a startup.

As your reputation gets noticed, you can then raise your pricing a little bit higher. The key idea is don't make it too expensive especially if you're just starting out as an ebook publisher. Bear in mind that hubris will make you fail easily, that's not what successful people are made of, just reminding you.

If you find the idea of establishing your own blog, or writing an ebook too tiring and exhausting to think of, you might want to consider blogging in existing "blog for payment" platforms. The best options for you would be sites like Medium, Hubpages, and Vocal.Media. Those platforms are popular, and have very high internet page-rankings.

Within them, you can discuss nearly any topic under, or over the sun. And if you are someone who is very well-versed with money-making especially in Forex, your ideas would be most welcome there. The good thing about writing on those platforms is there is no "audition drills" or something, you can just write and publish, although if you don't put some extra deep thought and effort into your articles, you might not get enough attention that can merit you with some earnings.

For Medium, you can get paid via audience claps. Meaning if a reader clicks "the clap" icon in your article, you could get paid up to $5 for each clap. Just imagine how much you can earn if a hundred readers clap on your single article!

With Hubpages and Vocal.Media, it's a bit different, you can get paid via advertising, much like you'd be with your own blog. The more viewers you attain with your articles, the higher your earnings would be. But take note, they are not the only blogging platforms out there! They're just mentioned here because by far, they are definitely the most popular of their kind.

There are also crypto-blogging websites that can really benefit from your trading knowledge. Even though Cryptocurrency is a bit different compared to Forex, the core concepts are actually the same. Many successful Forex investors are actually also hopping into the likes of Bitcoin and Ethereum. Since you have already understood solidly the ins and out of Forex trading, writing something about crypto coins shouldn't be that difficult.

You can just tweak you knowledge a bit, publish it in crypto-blogging platforms, and you can just wait for some additional dollars to get added to you already rising pile of income? Wait dollars? Yes, dollars. Most crypto-blogging sites today are run by a certain crypto-coin, but the equivalent money you'll get will be easily covertible to US dollars. Not all of them, but most of them basically works like that.

Here are the most popular crypto-blogging platforms today:

Steemit – Launched in 2016, it is the first of its kind. It is a micro-blogging social media site that's very similar to Twitter and Tumblr. Users can make money by posting articles that don't need to be very long, just enough to make other users be interested and give tips to the author. It is powered by cryto-coin Steem.

Hive.Blog – It has very notable similarities to Steemit. As a beginner, you can't post as often as you can as you need to buy more coins so you can make multiple posts. It was conceived when some users and co-owners of Steemit were disgruntled by how the latter was run. For the time being, many authors are earning with the same level as what they earned with Hive, as they are with Steemit.

Publish0x – Powered by Ethereum, it is currently the most attractive crypto-blogging site today. It enables you to post articles that are not your own, provided that you have the reprinting rights for those articles. You can also make money by just reading articles written by others, and also by giving tips. When you click on the tip button for each article, a portion of it goes to the writer, while a portion of it goes to your own wallet as well. For the time being, becoming a writer can only be achieved through application and invitation.

Read.Cash – It is the newest platform of its kind, and is declared as the closest cousin of Publish0x. When blogging for this platform, you will earn Bitcoin

Cash, which is currently the 4th-ranking crypto coin. The best thing about it is that even without too many views, you can still earn from the tips given by their software robot called "The Random Rewarder." By just showing hard work, you can earn some amounts everyday.

How much can you possibly earn in those platforms? Bloggers who have been around for quite some time in Steemit and Publish0x claim that by using platforms side by side, they have an average earning of $200 each month.

Not really a big amount, but here's the thing about cypto-blogging, you can post the same articles for each of them. So if you have 20 articles for Steemit, you can post the same for other similar sites as well, as long as you can prove that you're the author of those articles.

200 Dollars is just an average. But if you look at the top posts in Steemit or Hive, you can surely see that many authors are earning hundreds of dollars for just a single post. Most of these posts are about how to make money with cryptocurrency. Will your Forex articles be as attractive as those? Certainly, they will be.

What makes those platforms teem with users who read, give tips, and provide additional earnings is because they are always eager to learn about money-making. If you've earned some reputation with Forex already, you'd be most welcome there.

Even those who write about articles that are not related to trading are making great incomes with the likes of Publish0x and Read.Cash. Wouldn't you as a knowledgeable Forex trader make a higher stream of profits? Writing can be a very powerful tool, use it to rake in some passive income with your currency-trading knowledge.

By teaching Forex on video

"But I hate writing. Even though I love talking non-stop about Forex, I really hate the idea of having to write my knowledge and publish them on the internet!" Cool down friend, you can still make some extra income if you have that mode of thinking. How? By videoing yourself and explaining your trading adventures and techniques on screen.

The best way to achieve that would be to launch a Youtube channel. Much like launching your own blog, becoming a Forex vlogger would be very profitable too, although a bit much easier. People argue that anyone can write articles, but not everyone can shoot videos, edit them, and upload them online. Many of them actually think that vlogging is easier than blogging.

But the truth is, becoming a great writer, which is the key ingredient to blogging success is more difficult to master, than in becoming a great YouTuber. In becoming a good enough vlogger, you need to learn at least some basic videoing and editing skills. In addition of course to some communications skills.

You don't really need to talk like a TV host to attain vlogging success. Many YouTubers who can't even speak properly have a great number of viewers and subscriptions. To reinforce the idea further, it would be good to acknowledge that becoming a good vlogger requires you to watch a lot of videos.

But in becoming a good blogger, you need to read, and read a lot. Now which is easier, reading 50 books or watching 50 videos? Another reason why people are more attracted to becoming a vlogger than in becoming a blogger is that it's much easier to get an audience in the former.

Many Youtubers can attest to this. And many bloggers who are also vloggers can really be live witnesses that vlogging can get you a higher number of viewership quickly than with blogging. In Google, the average time for your blog to get searched and gain income is around 6 months. But within Youtube, your vlog could already gain viewership in just 24 hours.

It is estimated that a vlogger who has 1 million subscribers can earn up to $57,200 per year. But that could change though depending on where your channel is actively viewed from. With web advertising, the countries with the higher buying power actually pay more than those who just view ads but don't buy that much.

Another way by which you can share your knowledge through videos is by conducting webinars. By encouraging people to join your online discussions which of course needs promotion beforehand, you can ask them to put up some payment. Online courses are among the hottest money-making systems that are going on every day, endlessly on the internet. Many web-content publishers are getting extremely rich because of it, so to speak.

To help you set up a Forex webinar easily, Demio, WebinarJam, and Livestorm would be great platforms to check out. Youtube would be a great place to just conduct it too, although there are some strict requirements that you need to pass through to totally pull it off. The best way to get past that is to launch a channel with some attained viewership first. Once you've achieved that, conducting webinars should be fairly easier.

By podcasting and publishing audiobooks

But what if you just want to discuss your Forex knowledge but you hate to write, and also hate being videoed? Is there a way to make some extra income? Yes! – through podcasting or audiobook publishing. Witch such undertakings, all you need to have are just some guts, some good-enough speaking skills, a recording device such as your phone, and you're good to go.

While reading and watching videos might be the most-loved learning activities by a great number of people, there are those who prefer listening to instructional materials while they do their household chores or while they are out strolling in the park.

Research conducted by TheBestMedia website claims that, "If your podcast has about 10,000 downloads per episode, you can expect to make between $500 – $900 in affiliate sales. With audiobooks, voiceover artists who are just starting out can expect to earn $100 for each hour of finished audio. For industry veterans, those figures can reach up to $500 for a completed hour." That data is according to Business Insider.

Another brilliant option you can choose is by becoming a trading coach, or consultant. How you can make money out of that is by of course, establishing your web presence first. By setting up a Facebook or LinkedIn page that showcases your trading achievements, you can then put some promotional posts that should reach thousands of people for just a very small fee.

In Facebook, for instance, you can pay for an ad that could run for a week, which could reach up to 10,000 people, for as low as $3. How they would respond to that ad snippet is another story though. When you advertise your accomplishments as a Forex trader, the number of respondents greatly depends on your credentials: how many successful trades you already made in the past, and the rate at which your future trades could succeed... stuff like that.

Of course, becoming a productive trading coach or consultant could be very tiring and exhausting on your part, that's why extreme patience should come with the package as well. If you don't have the patience of a kindergarten teacher, maybe this gig is not for you. On the flipside though, many trading instructors are becoming richer too, in addition to their trading activities that they still do a lot.

As a trading coach, you'd be doing most of your tasks via phone calls, or via video conference apps. You need to have a steady setup of internet connection at home for this, alongside a reliable computer too. But all of that would just be irrelevant if you don't have the skills and conversational attitude that's the real important element for such an undertaking.

By Joining Forex Affiliate Programs

If you have established yourself as a Forex educator already via writing, videoing, or consultancy, you can actually make some more income by joining Forex affiliate programs. What are they? And how do they work?

The concept revolves around the idea that for every trader you can motivate into joining a certain Broker, you'll get paid with commissions. So basically, Forex Affiliations are those tasks that you do to promote or advertise an online brokerage firm so it can be made known to others.

For instance, check out In The Money Stocks, a company with a well-established affiliate program. They claim to have a 94% success rate in all their trading endeavors. By being an affiliate of theirs, you could earn $21 for each transaction. Another is Admiral Markets. The pay from their program is quite big, you could be paid up to $600 per client, and they take 0% commission from you. However, you need to have a deposit of $300 upon signing up.

Of course, they're not the only Forex Brokers with very good affiliate programs. There are literally dozens of them all over the internet. Search engines could really help you with that. Just make sure you've read enough reviews before putting your trust in any of them.

So far, those are the best methods by which you can earn by sharing your Forex trading knowledge on the internet.

By Taking Advantage of Forex Giveaways

Everybody loves free stuff. Who doesn't? When you're a bit exhausted with all the analyzing, speculating, and the over-all pressures trading has brought upon you, maybe you should exploit the giveaways that Forex enthusiasts can enjoy. They might not be money that you can add to your next trading capital, but they could be those tools that you can use to make the most out of your trading acts.

So what are those giveaways the likes of you and me from benefit from? They could be laptops, desktop PCs, cellphones, or some other handheld gadgets that you can connect to the internet with. Since trading can only be done with an internet connection nowadays, those who choose to hand over giveaways to various Forex traders took it upon themselves to give related equipment to them too.

So who are those generous people who are so willing to give us some free stuff? Most of them are actually Forex brokers and establishments with trading-related businesses. Technically, their very acts of giving free stuff that we can enjoy are nothing but advertisement tactics. For sure, nobody wants to give away something for nothing. When they offer you something, it means they usually want something in return from you too.

But most of the time though, those giveaways have no disadvantages whatsoever, except maybe for the annoyance that you'll get as those people will unleash their marketing tactics on you. Forex giveaways are there for the taking, you just have to know where to look.

Creating Wealth in 2021 and Beyond

As what's stated in the opening pages of this ebook, Forex has been through great changes already throughout the decades. We have to acknowledge that *in order to stay profitable within the market for the next years, we have to find other ways of attaining income from it.*

Whenever you Google up the long-tail keyword phrase "making money with Forex," all you will ever find are countless lists of articles that's about trading, which would be naturally so. Obviously, that's what Forex is all about, trading, trading, trading.

You've heard about overtrading being a bad habit. But is the idea of still making money with your Forex knowledge in a passive way, like when you're doing nothing at all so horrible? Not at all. In fact, many expert traders area still accumulating huge piles of wealth with their trading skills even when they are sleeping, literally. Because their knowledge are stored in internet content that people can access and study anytime, anywhere.

But what if you want to make money with Forex without actually trading? Can that be possible? Such would be a weird manifestation of one's curiosity. It would be like learning how to swim without immersing yourself in water. Sounds counter-intuitive, right? But here's something that might amaze you... you can really make money with Forex, without really trading... but by doing things that are just connected to it, in some ways.

So how can you still be an effective trader even in the next coming years? If only there's a crystal ball that we can look into for guidance, that would be extremely cool. Unfortunately, there is none. However, we can look into the following guides that can condition ourselves into becoming better and wiser traders.

Let us be clear though, the following tips and methods may not be about the very act of trading itself, you need to have acquired some pretty handful trading experiences along the way, in order for you to execute them properly and convincingly, Let's just say that the following are very cool side hustles with the wisdom that you got from your trading journey in this present year, and the years that await us.

6 Tips In Becoming an Effective Trader For The Years Ahead

1. Knowing about the future of money

Since money is one of the most important commodities in existence, its relevance to our daily lives in the future will still matter a lot. For that, we can be so sure of. As a trader who wishes to be even more productive in the years ahead, you have to take huge efforts in understanding how money will evolve.

Today, financial analysts, scientists, businessmen, and statisticians make predictions about how money-making will be like in the next decades or centuries. Do we really need to take great heed of those predictions? Yes. Though not to a very high extreme.

It is important for an effective trader to be aware of future trends. But from a realistic and practical standpoint, it wouldn't be wise to look too far ahead, because we might miss out on what really matters at these times, and in the next months as we go about on our trading endeavors. "Letting tomorrow worry about itself" might be a good mantra to remind yourself of occasionally, if you wish to balance things out between the now and the alter of trading.

For now, futurists seem to have this forecast that the likelihood of a "cashless society" will be more feasible. This was heralded by the arrival of the ATM and the debit card that goes with it. Since then, money-usage has never been easier and more convenient for people.

These days, mobile and internet banking are becoming more accessible for anyone. When cash cards became commonplace, they were only meant for the rich, but with online money-storage platforms like Paypal and Coinbase, anyone with very small amounts of money and an email address can take advantage of the benefits they're giving too. Since daily processes are digitized, cash became digitized too, which greatly diminished the very act of printing money and making metallic coins.

Then there's also online buying and selling. Even without spending real paper bills, people can now purchase products online and pay those items with just numbers that represent the actual money that they possess. In just a few clicks and confirmations with short phone calls, any product can be delivered to anyone's doorstep, without ever needing to deal with tangible cash.

In the next few years, it can be understood that the physical banks that we know today can be really obsolete. They're becoming irrelevant now, they could be totally gone not too long from now. Many financial analysts are declaring this us something that's inevitable. As a trader, you have to be aware that the future of money is digitization, and not understanding how digital cash works would be foolish idea.

From now on, try your best to learn about the likes of Paypal, Stripe, Payoneer, and anything similar. They could be the ultimate replacements of the banks where you deposit your money. Yes, it would be totally impossible to actually predict the future of money, but by looking carefully at how it is being managed now using digital technology, we can have a fairly reasonable assessment.

2. Earning by making a PAMM system

By far, this is the only technique here that's the most closely associated with an actual trading act. This is about letting people entrust a certain amount to you, so you can do the trading for them. All they need to do is hand you the money, and just let your magic fingers do the work. Of course, your success is also their success, which is also another way of saying that your failure is also theirs. Because nobody would ever trust a failing trader, you need to establish your reputation first before broadcasting into the world that you are a trader that they can wisely invest with.

The acronym actually stands for Percentage Allocation Money Management. Apart from Forex, such a kind of system has been applied in other business ventures as well. It has been known to really work in most cases, as long as done strategically by well-decisive businessmen.

In trekking into this, you need to explain to your clients clearly what happens if their investments win, or if their investments fail. You need to let them know what the risks are, and how high is the success or failure rate of your partnership. More often though, people who invest in this kind of system are those who expect that they would always win, so you need to really come up with a system that succeeds at all times, or at least, one that can be profitable for both parties.

Of course, this is quite hard to get by. The best way to implement this is by cutting down on the wins of the clients to a point in which they will have an almost fixed amount each time even if the wins are actually bigger than expected. This calls for some scenarios in which you will not totally reveal your trade secrets or methods to them although for sure, they would not love that.

The best thing to do is to always be transparent, so your renown as a businessman will not get damaged as you build your network within the trading business. The bottom line for this is that you need to emphasize and be very clear to the client about the percentages that you'll take from them, as payment for the trading efforts you pour out.

You do all the labor, but both parties will earn the rewards. Be very clear with that in accordance with reasonable transaction fees. By sorting that out fairly and squarely, your business endeavor should turn out just fine.

3. Studying Cryptocurrency

In the earlier chapters, we have compared Forex against the Stock Market as they are obviously 2 of the biggest money-making metaphorical machines in modern history. But we haven't talked that much yet about another major player – Cryptocurrency. Is it a threat to Forex? Very… and a very big threat at that, although it would be unfair for either major forces to pit them against each other.

Financial analysts bravely declare that since everything is going digital these days, the money will be ultimately digitized too in the not too distant future. Experts even claim that paper bills, coins, and even debit cards will vanish too because all you need to carry with you is your phone – which will act as your personal accountant as you buy, sell, and consume everyday commodities in your daily living.

Some even insist on outrageous claims that your money, as well as your entire identity, will be embedded into your wrist or forehead so that all the information about your being can be accessed whenever the need arises. This might happen, yes. But it would not be so until at least for another 100 years.

The point of such possible advancement is that money is really becoming digital. Without a doubt, cryptocurrency is the thing of the future, because it is the best proof that cash can really be transformed digitally. Businesses all over the world are now profiting efficiently as they are run by purely crypto coins alone.

As a smart trader, although you just deal within Forex, it would be foolish not to learn about Cryptocurrency. Even if we don't look upon it deeply, we can easily grasp that it has so many similarities with Foreign Currency Exchange. Crypto is taking the financial world by storm, and the force it's showing must never be belittled.

Since that can't be disputed, conventional trading wisdom hereby advises you that as you study about Forex, take another side course: learning about the likes of Bitcoin, Ethereum, and Ripple. They are 3 of the biggest name in the Cryptocurrency business, and they are surely the biggest players in that industry for the next foreseeable future.

4. Understanding the economy of China

Many people, especially those belong to the "western-category countries" hate this idea, but as a smart trader, you have to acknowledge that understanding the economy of the country known as "The Sun's Origin" – as their tagline is used by many journalists.

In case you haven't known it yet, China will be the next world power. Hate the idea as much as you can, but such an outcome is inevitable. Historians, political analysts, as well as world leaders, in general, have this separately unanimous conclusion that China will indeed be the most powerful nation on the planet in approximately less than 2 decades from now.

To reinforce this claim, let us delve a little into how a country becomes a world power. It's not because of the strength of a nation's army, or the number of citizens that live within it, but of the strength of its economy. That's how a country can gain global dominance, at least in this modern generation. Gone are the days when a nation needs to wage physical war against another nation to prove its power over the other.

Today, what needs to be done is to come up with a robust economy, one that can be effectively extended into other countries and continents. If a government can do that in the greatest measure compared to others, then that government is surely on its way to becoming the most powerful nation on the globe.

While it would be outrageous to expect that the Renminbi will gain supremacy over the Dollar and the Euro in the next few years, it will most likely be an equally strong currency force in the next decades. The best way to deal with this fact would be to study closely the economy of China in the same manner that you studied Europe's and the USA's.

Furthermore, acknowledging that Chinese-made products will be even more commonplace in the global market in the next set of years would be truly beneficial for a trader who wishes to be many steps ahead compared to common traders who rarely analyze things.

5. Understanding web-advertising

When Satoshi Nakamoto, the person behind the creation of Bitcoin came up with the idea of digitizing money, one of the main driving forces is computer networking technology – it is the very essence of the world's connectivity in this digital generation where we happen to exist. Now more than ever, the world is becoming smaller and smaller due to the existence of this digital universe called The Internet.

Even our beloved Forex. which can still dwarf out the crypto-giant easily is still highly dependent on the power of cyberspace to conduct business. And since it is one of the most important truths of all, a smart Forex trader needs to also learn a lot about web-advertising.

Like the business that revolves around television and radio broadcasting, websites heavily rely on advertising as well so that they can continue to exist on the web. Without the viewers and potential buyers of the products that those ads are showing, the internet will surely collapse under its own unimaginably heavy weight, though such mass is not to be taken from any physical sense.

Although web advertising has no direct thing to do with Forex just yet, it has now a lot of involvement already with how businesses in the world today are presented and made known to people. For that reason, a good trader must also be ever-ready to grasp the framework that makes internet advertising works so well.

6. Earning by becoming a Forex broker

When all the above methods fail, you could get into the last, but greatest resort of profitably earning with Forex without actually trading – becoming a broker yourself. Truth to be told, this is no small undertaking. Back in the days, all a Forex broker needs are a telephone line, an office, a set of record books, and some marketing skills. Today, however, you can't be like that anymore.

Forex brokers nowadays, literally all of them are modern-day offices equipped with high-end IT infrastructure. They are the kind of facilities that are almost exactly like those high-tech buildings you see in movies where humans are cloned or get transformed into superheroes. Okay, that might just be an exaggeration. But the truth is, you can't be a Forex broker today if you don't invest in expensive computer equipment with some technically savvy staff tasked to operate them.

Becoming a Forex broker is one of the most serious business endeavors you could ever hop into, that's why it's not actually meant for beginners. However, it should be something that you would want to think of from time to time because maybe, it could be the best direction for you as you get more experience and renown as a profitable Forex participant. This item is included here just to give answer to the question that pertains to making money with Forex without really trading.

The above-mentioned tips are a new set of methods. Take time on learning them because they are the best ways of *keeping ahead and in making additional income with Forex for this modern times of trading... and beyond.*

Parting Words For The Forex Aspirant

About 5 centuries ago, when the Europeans invested on building ships so they can embark on expeditions that can help them conquer the world, those who were the very first to partake on such an undertaking were declared as either "too ambitious" or "foolish" by people within their social circles. Centuries later though, we consider those people as heroes.

As you embarked on your first trading acts, you might have heard about people who are too dumb to understand what currency exchange is. By now, you could easily prove them wrong because as what you have understood already, trading can be a really profitable kind of business, one thing that can significantly change your life, in ways you never would have thought possible.

Whether or not you will take the habit of trading as a major part of your life is mainly up to you. You've been shown with the right mindset, the right tools, and the right guidance on how to take your first steps towards it. In addition, you've also been given proper directions which path to take in the future, as you continue the exciting and profitable life a Forex trader.

This book has been a good companion for you. While this might not be a totally complete guide that can make you fully understand the entirety of the currency market, it was a great motivator – for it surely did give you the right kind of ignition... to have that spark needed so you can be an efficient trader today, while there are still ripe trading fruits that you can pick and harvest.

Trends could rise really fast, and could fall even faster. That's why it is also very important that you remain updated with what's happening to the world, especially within the currency exchange market. Being well-versed with technology can really be a great help too – it is the ultimate tool that can help any businessman. It would be utterly foolish for anyone to endlessly wish to be rich, yet not planning on investing time to learn about how technology could be leveraged for the augmentation of someone's wealth.

To proceed further with your trading endeavors, it would be good to tap into the nearly-limitless resource that other, more experienced traders are giving to anyone who has access to online technology. Scour through Youtube, peek through the endless sea of blogs, and you will see multitudes of them. Some of them might not be that friendly, but most of them will surely provide you the help you need so you can become as smart as them, as you grow on your trading efforts.

Study their writings and listen to them carefully, you could end up just like those people. If you improve the techniques ans strategies they're giving, you could even be more profitable than they ever were. It just requires the proper mindset and since you have it already, things should be much easier now.

Hope you'll have the best of luck as you trek into your trading journey.